BEAUTIFULLY BROKEN

REEMA SUKUMARAN

BEAUTIFULLY BROKEN

Available from:
www.amazon.com

Scripture quotations marked ESV are from The Holy Bible, English Standard Version®, copyright © 2001 by Crossway, a publishing ministry of Good News Publishers. ESV® Text Edition: 2011. All rights reserved.

Scripture quotations marked NIV are from THE HOLY BIBLE, NEW INTER-NATIONAL VERSION®, NIV®. Copyright © 1973, 1978, 1984, 2011 by Biblica, Inc®. Used by permission. All rights reserved worldwide.

Project Management and Editing:
Grace Tesnau | The Write Design, LLC | gbrown@writedesignllc.com | 301-806-3669

Layout and Design (Cover and Interior):
Emily Harding | Harding Designs | hardingdesign@me.com | 803-746-7769

Stock Images:
istockphoto.com | shutterstock.com

Printed in the United States of America.

ISBN: 979-8-6952-3730-6

Sanj,
I dedicate this book to you.
It was with you that I learned to be me.
I love you.

ACKNOWLEDGMENTS

First and foremost, thank you Jesus for loving me as your favorite! Thank you for turning all the pain and hard times into blessings that I could not have imagined. I love you so much!

To each of my boys—Sammy, Tyler, Jordan, Max, Zach, and Josh— you are my world. In this book you are each mentioned just a few times and yet in life you are each endless volumes of joy to me. I love and adore you and I am so grateful God saw fit to bless me as your mom.

To my mom: I love you and miss you very much.

To my brothers, Kumar and Rajiv: If I had to pick who I would have by my side on this journey of growing up, I would pick you over and again. It has been a crazy ride and yet I am so grateful that we continue to be in this together. I love you both.

To Jayanta and Ujjal Gayen and Heather Cavanaugh: You filled my childhood with laughter and beautiful memories. I love you.

To David, Juliet, Jono, and Jess Knight: You will never know what a gift from God each of you are to me. I am so grateful for your love and family.

To Linda Agard and Ellen Jenkins: A girl could not ask for dearer friends who have been there for me through the decades.

To Shann Fanwar: Thank you for always having my back.

To Raj Sukumaran: You are my favorite brother-in-law! Thank you for all the rides to Ottawa, for lending a listening ear, and being someone I know will always there.

To Penny Welch, Jyoti Chandra, Christine Kathiravelu, Dorothy Thompson, and Sally Kater: You were there. You are there. I am blessed beyond measure with your love, care, and friendship.

To Shelley Sewell, Rhonda Motschiedler, Dianne Bigby, Sharon Stewart, Ziggy Gaines, Shirley Alonso, and Donna Perry: I have to specifically send my love to my Andrews girlfriends for all the love, joy, and memories we created together. Those years are some of my most cherished memories and I am so grateful to have shared them with you.

To Sharon Aka: I love how God has taken our friendship and used it in so many ways! From saving me and my dignity in the labor room, letting me be your roommate, being a shoulder to lean on when I needed one, to walking this path I am now on, I am so grateful for you and I love you.

To Pagie Isaac: Thank you for helping me do what no one else did.

To Trudy Morgan-Cole and Grace Tesnau: Thank you for helping me make this book what it is!

To the Seventh-day Adventist Church in Canada: Thank you for stepping up and being like Jesus. Thank you for hearing my pain and offering me a path toward healing (though my pain was no fault of your own). Grace Macintosh, you are one of God's angels here on earth. Thank you for shining God's love to the hurting and being willing to hear and follow His voice.

To my therapist: I can only say "Thank You," despite knowing that it is not enough.

PREFACE

"WHO SPILLED THE MILK?!!"

His rage was triggered. His voice escalated as he lost control. I sat between my younger brothers, Rajiv, age eight, and Kumar, age five, so relieved that it was not me. I had not spilled the milk, but my heart was still racing. I felt so bad for my brothers. My dad asked again. Then one of my brothers looked over at me and said, "DeeDee spilled it."

I was shocked and speechless at first. My dad ordered me to stand up and come to him. Frightened, I sobbed, "It wasn't me! I didn't spill the milk!!"

Consumed as he was by his rage, my dad abandoned all reason. As I continued to beg him to listen and believe me, he grabbed a wooden spoon.

"Give me your hands!!"

I put my hands out, palms up, and the spoon came down. SMACK!!

He hit my palm with a force that the ten-year-old me, not even sixty pounds, could not imagine surviving. Then he smacked my second palm with increased ferocity. As he beat me over and over, I cried out, "I didn't do it! It wasn't me!!"

Finally, mercifully, the wooden spoon broke on my tiny hands. I assumed that would be the end, but I was wrong. Unless I admitted that I HAD spilled the milk, he was not going to stop.

Still sobbing, I falsely confessed. "It was me! I spilled the milk!!" Surely if I admitted it and apologized, the beating would stop.

I was wrong again. My dad apparently then decided that I needed to be taught a lesson about lying. The wooden spoon broken, he grabbed the first thing he could use to inflict pain and teach me an invaluable lesson that I would never forget.

"I'm going to thrash you!!" he yelled, as he hit me with a metal fly swatter that left welts on my arms and thighs.

I'm not sure how long the beating lasted. It seemed endless. I realized he was not going to stop any time soon and I could no longer withstand the pain. Death seemed like the only way to make the nightmare end, so I cried out, "Just kill me, Daddy! Just kill me!"

CONTENTS

BEGINNINGS

CHAPTER ONE

"The best and most beautiful things in the world can't be seen or even touched. They must be felt with the heart."
—Helen Keller

Pijush Kiron Dikshit was born in East Bengal on June 23, 1934, one of seven children, (two sisters and four brothers). Due to circumstances beyond his family's control, Pijush and a brother ended up on the streets in their early teens, often getting into trouble and heading toward a life of crime. In his later teens, Pijush was discovered by a group of Christians who were holding a series of meetings where his father worked as the interpreter. The evangelist suggested that Pijush and his brother attend a Christian college in Puna and facilitated this by arranging boarding and covering the finances.

Pijush worked as a colporteur, selling religious books, and he did other odd jobs while he was in school. He was a gregarious extrovert and enjoyed being the center of attention. Though he was not a natural student, he was able to make a good living as a colporteur and he enjoyed the constant interaction with people.

Aside from these few facts, I don't know much about my dad's early life. He preferred to share folktales and myths from Indian culture rather than talk about his own childhood and youth.

Gloria Eswar Rao was born on August 21, 1936 in Nuzid, India, to Eswar Rao and Kamala Madirala. My grandmother, Kamala, had lost her parents as a child and lived with her uncle for a time. It was common in Indian villages at this time for girls to be married at a young age. My grandmother was married at the age of 12 or 13 to my grandfather, who was seven years her senior. My mom, Gloria, was the fourth of their six children, one boy and five girls; one girl died at the age of three due to sickness.

My mom often said that she had a wonderful childhood. She and her siblings were raised in a God-fearing home. My mom idolized her father, who was a minister and worked for the church. She admired the type of man he was and his love for God. His example would be emulated in how she lived her life.

My mom and her siblings helped with the household chores as my grandmother, a child herself, grew up while raising her own children. My mom had a playful spirit and found joy in the little things. I love a picture I once saw of my mom swinging on a tree branch, laughing. She and her siblings were close as children and remained close, talking every day in her later years. She was a natural caretaker and continued to care for others throughout her life.

Though the family was close, one thing made my mom unhappy: her complexion was dark, and she viewed this as a curse. She felt ugly. To make matters worse, my mom felt that her mother was partial to her sisters, who were lighter-skinned, and in my mom's eyes, prettier. Until her final days, my mom still bemoaned her complexion and talked about how she was mocked and teased about her looks.

My grandfather died at the young age of 57. My mom's connection to her father had always been deep. He knew she was picked on and that she was not her mom's favorite child. But he loved her and cherished her, and he asked her to take care of her mother in a special way. Throughout her life, my mom kept her father on a pedestal and treasured her memories of him.

CHAPTER TWO

"We must accept finite disappointment,
but we must never lose infinite hope."
—Martin Luther King Jr.

In 1966, my parents were introduced to each other at a friend's wedding. Almost immediately, my dad began courting my mom aggressively. She was already 30 years old and felt pressure to accept my dad's courtship. He was of the same faith, he was charming, and her friends encouraged her to pursue the relationship.

But after they dated for a while, things began to change. My dad became emotionally abusive toward my mom, taunting her dark skin and "ugliness." "Who else would want you?" he would ask her. He saw her insecurities and played on those. When she attempted to end the relationship, he would beg for forgiveness and promise to change. When she tried to leave him again after his repeated misbehavior, my dad threatened suicide and she caved in out of fear.

A week or so before their wedding, my mom confided in her father that she did not want to go through with the marriage. She told him the truth about their relationship, and her father promised to help her. Sadly, he had a major heart attack and passed away just days before the wedding.

Devastated and heartbroken at the loss of her beloved father, defeated and feeling trapped, my mother walked down the aisle, promising her future to a man who had already shown a side of himself that was unacceptable. Their wedding pictures are such a contradiction: my dad is happy and smiling for all to see, while my mom's face is full of sadness and heartache.

As they settled into married life, my dad's abusive behavior continued. He seemed to enjoy hurting my mom any chance he could. He threw the women of his past in her face, telling her that *she* was the lucky one, because he could have had his pick of any of them. Though my mom had grown up with a loving father, her lack of self-esteem played a huge part in the choices she made. She believed her husband's lies.

Within their first year of marriage, my mom was pregnant, but sadly, she lost that baby. Shortly after, she became pregnant with me. In September 1968, I came into the world as Reema, and my parents had the thrill of holding me for the first time. My dad was so excited that he picked me up and tried to carry me out of the hospital before we were discharged. Obviously he wasn't allowed to leave with me, but he was just so eager to take me home that he couldn't think straight. I was adored and cherished as I entered the world.

My mom was diagnosed with breast cancer shortly after I was born. Her doctors recommended a double mastectomy, a life-altering decision. She trusted the competence of the doctors, and specifically a doctor who was her close friend. After the removal of her breasts, it was discovered that the lump was benign. It was just one more unfortunate incident in what would turn out to be a life filled with struggles and hardship.

My mom had the luxury of staying home during these early years, as my dad was bringing home a good income from colporteuring. We had a nice little set-up, with some servants to help my mom with some of the household tasks. This allowed her to enjoy motherhood. Sadly, this situation did not last very long.

My dad continued the emotional abuse that had begun during their courtship, mocking my mom with jabs about her dark skin and telling her that she was ugly. He taunted her with threats of abandoning their marriage. And his emotional abuse would soon give way to physical abuse.

I began experiencing my dad's abuse when I was just one year old. I was playfully hitting him on his head, and without warning this set him off. He yelled that I was to never raise my hand to him ever again and knocked my head hard with his knuckles. My mom was appalled that he would hurt his baby. She reprimanded him, which caused him to berate her for undermining his authority.

Little things upset him when dealing with me as a baby. When I tugged at a toy being played with by another child my dad would become furious at my behavior. He would yell at me for being selfish and not sharing and then spank me to teach me a lesson.

He was erratic with his affection. He was so proud of me and loved to show me off; he showered me with love, especially when other people were around. Yet in private, especially when I needed care, he was hands-off. My mom was the one who mothered me, doted on me, and took care of all the necessary things.

Life with my dad was very unpredictable for my mom as well. He never courted her or did nice things for her. Instead, he seemed to find enjoyment in making her feel insufficient and unworthy of love. Despite this, my mom always took time and thought to please him. She spent hours making meals the way he preferred, only to have him push the food away and ask for something totally random instead. She was berated for making the meals too salty, or not salty enough. He never acknowledged the love she put into preparing his meals.

My dad's anger slowly escalated from verbal reprimands to physical displays of rage, where he would throw or break things. My mom cowered. Whatever the grievance, she made sure I was out of harm's way, and then, with her slim hands protecting her face, she would beg him to stop, crying out an apology.

While things were far from ideal inside our home, my parents also faced pressure from outside. Christians were not received well in this area of India. Christians who shared their faith jeopardized their personal safety. A missionary family who lived a short way from us had their child kidnapped, killed, and left at their doorstep. One day as my dad was working, he was approached by some men who warned him, "Turn around and leave! If we see you again, we will cut you up and kill you!" My dad was terrified and ran off. After a short distance, he looked over his shoulder, grateful to see the men had disappeared.

In 1970, my parents made the decision to move to Canada.

CHAPTER THREE

"You never know how strong you are
until being strong is your only choice."
—Bob Marley

My brother Rajiv was born on my second birthday. Rajiv and I hated sharing the same birthday! But because we were both born via C-section, my mom was able to pick that date.

We left India in 1970, just after Rajiv was born. My dad's sister and her family had settled in Toronto, Canada a couple of years earlier, and my parents followed suit with Rajiv and me. Initially we stayed with my aunt, uncle, and their two boys, who were two and four years old. We all grew up more like siblings than cousins.

Soon we moved into an apartment right next door to these cousins.

My mom got a job as a nurse at the hospital directly across from our apartment complex. My dad also worked at the hospital, doing menial work. My parents' shifts overlapped by an hour. My mom would wake me up—I was three years old—and sit me on the sofa, placing my one-year-old brother beside me. She would turn on "Sesame Street" on the television and then leave. I knew how to change Rajiv's diaper. I knew how to comfort him if needed. We were left alone in the apartment for that hour with the knowledge that my aunt was in the apartment next door.

I asked my mom in later years if my memory of this time was correct, and she confirmed that it was. With my aunt living next door, she knew I could go there if I needed help.

While my mom was a registered nurse in India, she had to pass the boards to be certified in Canada. Passing the boards required studying, since the terminology, policies, and procedures were all different. My mom also worked double shifts. My dad, realizing that my mom could make decent money, quit his job at the hospital and went back to working as a colporteur. This allowed him to work when the mood struck him. From this point on, he left the financial responsibility to my mom—the money she brought home had to cover all the bills.

Shortly after moving to Canada, my parents realized our last name, Dikshit, came with issues. In India, the name was common and did not have the same connotation as in North America. My dad's first name, Pijush, also had some negative connotations, but he didn't seem to mind. Early on during his time in Canada, my dad joked, "I am not orange juice; I am not apple juice; but I am dirty Pee-Juice!" I heard this for years and he never got tired of sharing that joke; he had no shame about it at all. Thankfully, around the time I began elementary school, my dad changed our last name from Dikshit to Dixit. And despite his many jokes, soon after that, Pijush had his own name legally changed to Peter Dixit.

I have fond memories of my dad during those early years. He was often fun-loving, and I loved him very much. He would crawl on all fours, giving me a horsey ride, or playing house with me. Sometimes I was even lucky enough to get a piggyback ride from him. Now, even five decades later, I have vivid memories of holding my dad's hand as we walked, feeling safe and loved by him.

In those early years it was easy for me to believe that ours was a happy home. At that age I was oblivious to the heartbreaking ugliness that would soon taint my childhood memories. Years passed before my mom told me the story of the time my dad hit me on my head with his fist when I was just a year old. But by the time I was five years old, my memories of my dad were clouded by his unpredictable raging temper.

My parents found their niche with friends in Toronto, many of whom had been classmates of theirs in India. But many of these friendships didn't last, because my dad manipulated things so that he came between my mom and her friends. He hated not being the center of her attention, even for a short time. He would tell lies about her to friends and family. It became so embarrassing that my mom eventually withdrew from her circle of friends.

My dad hosted dinners for his friends, with my mom, who was an amazing cook, doing all the work. She could make anything taste like a five-star meal. Even the pride she might have felt in her cooking, my dad would steal from her. As everyone began to eat, he would always say, "If you like the food, thank me; if not, tell my wife!"

At the time, I never thought about how this might feel to my mom. I can only imagine the hurt she must have felt. My mom never had much self-esteem. She was plagued by her darker skin, which was considered a deficit in her world, where lighter skin represented more beauty. She had no one in her life to shower her with affection or compliments, and over time she believed the lies my dad sowed. She often told the story of my birth and how she was asked whether I was her sister's baby, the implication being that she could not have given birth to a fair-skinned baby like me. The fact that my dad was of lighter skin tone seemed to have been overlooked.

I was five years old when my mom became pregnant again. On one of her visits to her doctor, he realized that she was in an abusive marriage. He told her, "You and your children are not in a safe situation. You don't have to live like this—you need to tell someone."

It was the only time my mom ever reached out for help. She told a family member about my dad's abuse. Without missing a beat, that person's response to her was: "We do not leave our spouse. You need to deal with it."

That was in 1973. Never once in the next twenty years did she seek a way to escape her nightmare. It took such bravery to share this deep dark secret of hers and when that was shut down, my mom never spoke up again. It makes me furious to think of the pain we all lived with because of that selfish, thoughtless, unkind response.

CHAPTER FOUR

"The world breaks everyone, and afterward,
some are strong at the broken places."
—Ernest Hemingway

On November 16, 1973, my youngest brother, Kumar, was born. Despite my disappointment at not getting a sister, I quickly fell in love with this baby. Kumar and I developed a close bond early in life. Rajiv and I were true siblings, being two years apart, but to Kumar I became a second mom, as my mom had to work so much to support us. At the age of five, I was able to feed, change, and play with Kumar. My dad was very little help, even when he was home.

With time, my dad became more volatile. We learned to tiptoe around him, never knowing when he would erupt.

He often bartered for things in return for the books he was supposed to sell. This made more work for my mom, as her pay also had to cover the bills my dad accumulated for the books he bartered instead of sold. One of the things he brought home was a 50-gallon fish tank. He loved this tank and enjoyed the upkeep. One afternoon, after he had spent hours cleaning the tank, he went to take a shower. While our dad was in the shower, Rajiv pushed a chair up to the tank, wanting to be helpful by feeding the fish.

At that moment, my dad came out with a towel wrapped around his waist, just in time to see my brother ready to put food into the tank.

My dad startled him with a yell and Rajiv ended up dumping all the food into the tank. My dad was furious! Rajiv ran to him and cried, "Sorry Daddy, I was just trying to help feed the fish." Three-year-old Kumar also ran to my dad and grabbed his towel, begging him to not spank Rajiv. The towel began to slip, and our dad had to grab it to save his dignity. We all started to giggle. It was one of the rare times when my dad's anger was defused and he was able to see the humor in the situation, rather than losing his temper.

We lived for the moments when he relaxed and had fun with us. Sometimes he would make a tent out of sheets and have us take our afternoon nap in there. When he decided to wash the kitchen floor, he would wet it, add soap, and let us slide around as we delighted in the mess, our laughter bouncing off the walls.

But in a split second, his sanity could vanish. Once we were in the strip mall across from our apartment, buying some groceries after school. As we rode home in the car, the after-school meltdown began and the three of us started bickering, tired and hungry after a long day. My dad lost it. He screamed that he was going to kill us. Driving toward the light pole that was in the center of the parking lot, he threatened: "I am going to smash right into that pole and kill you all!"

We didn't know at the time that my dad suffered from a significant mental illness. In the 1970s much less was known and understood about this, and especially in immigrant communities, it was rarely discussed. Even later in his life, when this knowledge was more common, he was never able to acknowledge his own mental illness. How much different all our lives would have been if his illness had been understood and treated!

Obsessive Compulsive Disorder (OCD) was one of my dad's struggles. We were taught at a young age that things needed to be precise. Towels were to be centered with the exact space on each side of the towel holder. Shoes were to be lined up neatly as soon as we walked into the apartment. My brothers' hairline parts were to be exact and straight, something they would come to me for help, fearing the repercussions from a messed-up hair part. Our Bibles were never to have anything placed on top of them. To this day, I still cringe when

I see a Bible buried under stuff; it seems so disrespectful.

My dad thrived on dominating us. His dominance was based on fear—our trepidation that our actions might precipitate his next eruption. Yet, terrorizing my mom still seemed to be his favorite pastime. This happened mostly in the car.

He would comment on the smallest thing while driving, such as a bird in his sight, ask my mom if she saw it, and then ask *her* to point it out to him, as if every interaction was a test she had to pass. He seemed to derive pleasure from watching the fear and stress flood her face. He was so controlling and demeaning that he sucked the enjoyment out of a simple drive. The easiest way to describe my dad's behavior toward my mom in these situations is that he was a bully.

The biggest nightmare was navigation! Folded paper maps, the kind you needed to be a cartographer to decipher, were always the catalyst of impending doom. My mom was educated and intelligent, but her nerves were no doubt shot whenever she was asked to look at a map. Those maps … again, who knew how to use them? Half the time, they were upside down, or the print was too small. And who could determine north, south, east, or west? Nine times out of ten my dad would pull over, and with his voice accentuating each word, he would point out what he deemed her stupidity.

I loved the little smug smirk on my mom's face when my dad eventually had to stop to ask for directions. She and I had a special connection, even when I was very young. She would give me the "Shhh, stop" look before my dad noticed.

I didn't know that my childhood was different from anyone else's. In the early 1970s it was not uncommon to see teachers using a paddle or belt on a student in the hallway at school. I saw "beatings" as just part of our reality. I saw other parents "lose it" with their children and beat them past what we would now call appropriate, so I had no idea what "inappropriate" was.

One day Kumar, who was then four years old, was drawing or doodling during church rather than listening to the pastor. When we got home, Dad felt compelled to give him a spanking. He raised his hand and his palm came down to make contact on my brother's bottom. But it was my dad, not my brother, who reacted with a yelp. Kumar had put a book in the backside of his pants, and my dad's palm received a good sting! This escalated Dad's temper, and he whipped my brother. He then ordered Kumar to go in the hallway of our apartment and stay there and ask Satan to leave his heart. Despite the repercussions, a giggle comes out when I remember my dad's hand connecting with that book.

Our community included a mix of Canadian-born families as well as immigrants, and my school friends were also my neighbors. We would walk to school and back, then play outside until the streetlights came on. In the summer, my brothers and I were often left alone while my dad headed to work, or wherever he went. By this time, I was about ten or eleven, and able to do what needed to be done around the house and for my brothers. We could play all we wanted, but my dad would leave us with math multiplication tables or other things that he expected us to memorize by the time he returned. We knew better than to disobey; harsh consequences were sure to follow if we didn't do as he said.

When I was in fifth grade, Kumar was in half-day kindergarten. With my mom at work and my dad out, our babysitter was supposed to take Kumar home until Rajiv and I got out of school. One day, Kumar threw a fit and for some reason refused to go with the sitter. Instead, he joined me in class; a chair was pulled up to my desk and this somehow seemed normal. My teacher had a young daughter who stayed in class with her after kindergarten, so she may have understood my mom's predicament. The boy who sat beside me put Elmer's glue on Kumar's hand and showed him how, after letting it dry, it looked like skin when you peeled it off. It gave my little brother something to do to amuse himself.

I look back and wonder how my mom did it. How did she survive those years with us as little ones and toddlers? She never complained about the hand she was dealt. She trusted and looked to God for her strength, but she also relied on me a great deal.

A "parentified child" is defined as a child who becomes a "parent" to their own parents and younger siblings. When I learned this term in counseling years later, I realized how perfectly it described my role in our family from a very young age. I became a partner to my mom, her confidant and friend. I was a parentified child.

After we had lived in Toronto for seven or eight years, my dad and his sister made the decision to invite their mother in India to come live with us in Canada. My dad's father had died shortly after I was born. Thakuma, as we affectionately called my grandmother, came to live with us. I was happy to have her with us, even though she did not speak English. There was a bond that crossed the language barrier. I never really felt like I got to know her well, but I am grateful for that season. The Canadian weather was a big adjustment, but I believe she could have adapted to life in Canada if she had found some happiness in our home.

I'm not sure what memories my Thakuma had of my dad as a young man, but it was likely that he was not the same man by the time she lived with us. He was controlling and quick tempered. One memory seems to sum it all up. We were at Lake Ontario, out in the cold gusty wind. My dad wanted a picture of my mom and Thakuma together. It was something neither of them wanted to do; they wanted to get back into the warm car. I don't remember my dad's words, only the ugliness of his tone as he forced them to pose for the picture neither of them wanted. Thakuma and mom's faces were so dejected. Needless to say, my Thakuma returned to India, likely doing a happy little jig upon returning to her home. Yet she must have had a heavy heart as she witnessed what her son had grown up to be.

CHAPTER FIVE

"Don't cry over spilled milk."
—Benjamin Franklin

In the middle of my fifth-grade year, my parents decided to move to the United States. The week before we headed to Orlando, Florida, my mom went to the hairdresser and cut her long flowing hair into a very short style. It was one of the few times when she just did what she wanted, not caring whether my dad approved or not. She also stopped wearing saris, the traditional Indian dress. I still have some aunts who continue to wear saris every day despite living in North America for more than fifty years. But my mom found her style and some freedom in pants and blouses.

When I look back at my childhood, the three years we lived in Orlando were some of my happiest times, despite the drama that was woven into our family life. We first moved into a little apartment complex with a community pool where my brothers and I spent many hot days splashing around. There was also a lake behind our complex with rumors that an alligator or two would bask in the sun near the water. Our childish curiosity made us brave enough to venture out just slightly behind the back of the apartment to see if we could spot these creatures, but fear sent us running back squealing, without getting too close to the lake.

A couple of friends from church lived in the same building, and we played outside most of the day, coming in only to eat. Kraft Dinner was a staple for us at lunch, as that was something I could make whenever my dad was off doing his own thing, which seemed to be most afternoons.

That apartment was the setting of a painful memory, permanently etched in my mind. I was about ten years old, shortly after we moved to Orlando. My mom, who worked the 7:00 a.m. to 3:00 p.m. shift, was already gone. My dad typically made breakfast for us every morning. This particular morning, we each had a glass of milk with our meal. My dad, with his compulsion for order, warned us about spilling the milk. We had probably done so one too many times and he was through with that mess. But his warning made us nervous, and the inevitable happened.

"WHO SPILLED THE MILK?!!"

His rage was triggered.

His voice escalated as he lost control. I sat at the table between my younger brothers, Rajiv, age eight, and Kumar, age five, so relieved that it was not me. I had not spilled the milk, but my heart was still racing.

I felt so bad for my brothers. My dad asked again. Then one of my brothers looked over at me and said, "DeeDee spilled it."

I was shocked and speechless at first. My dad ordered me to stand up and come to him. Frightened, I sobbed, "It wasn't me! I didn't spill the milk!!"

Consumed as he was by his rage, my dad abandoned all reason. As I continued to beg him to listen and believe me, he grabbed a wooden spoon.

"Give me your hands!!"

I put my palms out and the spoon came down. SMACK!!

He hit my palm with a force that the ten-year-old me, not even sixty pounds, could not imagine surviving. Then he smacked my second palm with increased ferocity. As he beat me over and over, I cried out, "I didn't do it! It wasn't me!!"

Finally, mercifully, the wooden spoon broke on my tiny hands. I assumed that would be the end, but I was wrong. Unless I admitted that I HAD spilled the milk, he was not going to stop.

Still sobbing, I falsely confessed. "It was me! I spilled the milk!!" Surely if I admitted it and apologized, the beating would stop.

I was wrong again. My dad apparently then decided that I needed to be taught a lesson about lying. The wooden spoon broken, he grabbed the first thing he could use to inflict pain and teach me an invaluable lesson that I would never forget.

"I'm going to thrash you!!" he yelled, as he hit me with a metal fly swatter that left welts on my arms and thighs.

I'm not sure how long the beating lasted. It seemed endless. I realized he was not going to stop any time soon and I could no longer withstand the pain. Death seemed like the only way to make the nightmare end, so I cried out, "Just kill me, Daddy! Just kill me!"

My words stopped him in his tracks, jolting him out of his rage. He stopped beating me, saying only, "I hope you learned your lesson."

My plea for him to kill me must have made an impact; he repeated my words to my mom. I never knew what my mom thought, or if she spoke up in my defense. The welts and marks on my body reminded me that my dad's touch was not to be trusted. I yearned for the gentle loving hand that once held my little hand in his, but I knew I couldn't trust him. I never knew when rage would overtake him.

My mom never replaced the wooden spoon that my dad broke across my hands that day, even after we all eventually left home. I love cooking with a wooden spoon, yet even still today I often pause as I look at that kitchen utensil and wonder: what kind of ugliness could fill a heart, to break a piece of wood on a little girl—his own flesh and blood?

As violent as my dad could be, he could sometimes be the polar opposite. I cherished memories such as the time when I was sick with a high fever and my dad filled the bathtub up for me to cool off, prepared food for me, and made me feel safe and comforted. The times my dad stepped out in love were moments I clung to, but they didn't erase the memory of his rage or his violence.

Years later, one of my brothers admitted to spilling the milk. How must he have felt, watching as my dad thrashed me? Both of my little brothers had begged my dad to stop beating me, with tears streaming down their baby faces. None of us ever forgot that day.

SURVIVAL

CHAPTER SIX

"Life becomes easier when you learn
to accept the apology you never got."
—Robert Brault

A year after moving to Orlando, our family rented an apartment in one of the hospital-owned employee housing sites. This move was perfect for me, as my best friend lived there too. The apartment building had four units that formed a U-shaped complex with a playground on the property. Memories of carefree summers roller skating up and down the sidewalk, making forts in a little wooded area that seemed like a forest to us, or playing at the park just down the road, are among my favorites of this time. But our lives were still overshadowed by my dad's unreasonable rage.

The laundromat for our apartment building was located toward the end of the complex. Laundry was something my dad usually did, as it relaxed him. I learned at a very young age how to fold clothes in the specific way he insisted on having them folded. As with everything, we learned to do it right or else there would be consequences.

One summer day, my dad instructed me to put the clothes in the washing machine, then the dryer, and once finished, bring them back to our place and fold them. That was easy enough to do in between roller skating up and down the sidewalk, playing with my brothers and friends. I paused to put the clothes in the dryer and eventually, when they were dry, I took them to the apartment, folded them, and continued to play.

My dad came home and, upon glancing at the laundry that I had folded and left in the basket, hollered for me to come into the apartment. That tone was there, the one that gave me goosebumps. My heart thundered and I struggled to hold back tears. I climbed the stairs, racking my brain and wondering what I had done wrong.

My dad was furious at me. "I told you to bring in the laundry—why didn't you do it?"

"I did bring in the laundry," I insisted.

"All of it?"

I thought I had brought in all the laundry. My dad made me walk down to the laundromat with him and check the washers. It turned out there was another load of laundry there that I had not seen.

As we walked back to our place, he told me that he was going to teach me another lesson that I would never forget. He beat me. With each smack of the belt on my bottom and legs, he emphasized each word. "WHEN. YOU. DO. A. JOB. DO. IT. THOROUGHLY! DO. YOU. UNDERSTAND?"

"I'm sorry! It was an accident!"

None of that mattered to my dad. My apology fell on deaf ears. There was no excuse or tolerance for mistakes like this.

I was furious. The pain that he inflicted physically was enough to make me mad, but I was angrier about the fact that it *was* a mistake. Did he not make mistakes? Did anyone beat him when he did? I was a good kid. I was asked to do things that kids my age never had to do. He had no right to punish me for something that was an honest mistake.

For supper that evening my dad took us to Pizza Hut. This was an extravagant treat for us, and it was also my dad's version of an apology. I was sitting across from him in the booth, but I was still not able to just let it go. The only way I could retaliate was with silence. I could not outright be rude, so I did speak when spoken to, but I was still angry at him, and he could see the passive-aggressiveness simmering within my small frame.

My mom looked at me, moving her head ever so slightly. Her body language begged me to let it go. So often I did things simply to please my mom. My dad, reading my body language and recognizing my anger, quietly passed me a $20 bill across the table. That was also huge in our world and certainly not a common occurrence. I accepted the peace offering, realizing this was a rare token of my dad seeking my acceptance and reaching out to me. In that moment it was almost enough to make me to believe he was sorry and that maybe, just maybe, he loved me.

CHAPTER SEVEN

"If you could reason with religious people,
there would be no religious people."
—House

Life at home was dominated by religion. While my parents were not very involved with our school, our involvement with the church was the major focus of our family's life. My best friend and my cousins were my social circle. We did everything together. Pathfinders, our denomination's version of the Boy Scouts and Girl Scouts, was a huge part of our lives. We went on camporees, competed for honor badges to add to our sashes, and learned all sorts of life lessons. The leaders of our Pathfinder Club were a lovely couple who had an RV and lived on a lake. Their life seemed so cool to my twelve-year-old self. I've never forgotten their love and kindness. Looking back, I wonder if they saw past our family's facade to the turmoil that hovered over us, just a blink away.

Church was a place where my dad felt he was someone, where he was treated with respect and accepted. It was a safe place for us too, knowing that when my dad was happy we were allowed to be happy as well.

Our home was full of religion. Over the summer, my dad would give us Bible verses and instruct us to have the texts memorized by the time he returned. We had learned over the years that there were repercussions for not learning them. These were not short texts like John 11:35—"Jesus wept"—but entire chapters, like 1 Corinthians 13.

We had family worship every day. First, we sang songs, and my siblings and I would find ways to annoy each other with our song choices. One of us would always pick "Father Abraham," knowing it would irritate the other siblings as it was endless and included crazy actions, which my dad would make us stand up and do. We would pick "Teach Us to Love, Lord" because one of the verses said, "If I grow fat, Lord, someone grows lean/Don't let me put my brother down, like some that I've seen." I have no clue what our definition of "fat" was, seeing as we were all thin as rails!

We actually had a songbook that my dad put together called "The Dixit Family Songbook." We didn't know until many years later that the lyrics my dad had written down were often nothing like the words everyone else sang. They were just the words my dad made up or thought he knew. He spent an incredible amount of time on this project, often paying someone to type the pages upon pages of songs. This was another one of his obsessions, something he worked on over the years.

Each of us also had a copy of a devotional book that my dad would read from, and we were expected to follow along. At any point, he could stop and ask one of us what the next word was, and if we didn't know or took too long to answer, he would lay into us for not paying attention. He would warn that if he asked again, and we were not following, we would get it. We struggled to focus in the best of times, so this was excruciating.

My dad blamed my mom for corrupting us by allowing us to watch TV shows like *Little House on the Prairie.* He told her she was the reason we were not good children; he told us that the devil was in us and that we would not be going to heaven. He never seemed pleased with any of our accomplishments or anything about us.

We eventually left the hospital housing and rented a house in what I considered a "real neighborhood." The outside of the house was pink with grey trim and shutters. There was the typical overhang for a garage and a cute little yard. The inside was an average three-bedroom home, and then there was an add-on room, a large empty space with a stage of sorts. While my parents were getting ready for church we would often hang out in this room, with my brothers preaching sermons as they pretended to be pastors.

That given a chance to perform on a stage, my brothers immediately thought to pastor, indicates how important religion was to our family. Because of this, we were very restricted with what we were and weren't allowed to do. We could go to a lake with friends and family, but because it was Sabbath (our day of rest), we were not allowed to go into the water, despite the fact that we were sweltering under the Florida sun. My brother Kumar often found ways to bypass such rules, for example, by "accidentally" falling into the water. On the Sabbath we weren't allowed to ride our bikes or play with things that we would have used during the week.

Despite being away from his motherland, my dad really missed India and found ways to bring India into our lives. He took worship songs from his mother tongue, Bengali, and translated the words for some of the songs into English, so we could learn these Bengali songs. My aunt played the harmonium, a small pump organ kind of instrument; one cousin would play the tablas, which are Indian drums played by sitting on the floor and playing with both hands. Another cousin played the accordion. We would meet on Friday nights, have supper together, and then my dad would teach us these songs and the tunes.

This in and of itself might seem an ordinary occurrence for an immigrant family, but, as always, my dad took things to the next level. He took the show on the road, going to nursing homes to perform for the seniors there. My aunt and uncle owned a retirement home, so this was where we first performed our little show. My dad was in his element, chatting away with the folks about the instruments, explaining the meaning of the songs, and sharing stories of his memories in his motherland.

This was tolerable the first or second time, but as budding teenagers, we did not see singing Bengali worship songs at the nursing home as "cool." We felt like we were being held hostage, forced to perform our little show week after week, with no choice about whether we wanted to participate or not. We were given little passages of scripture to recite. In the spirit of true teenage rebellion, the eye rolling and mumbling were often in full effect among the hostages. When we were caught in the act, my siblings and I received the stare of death or the threat of bodily harm.

The forced performances at nursing homes and hospitals and the threat of violence that lay behind those shows, all illustrated the gap between religion and true spirituality in our home. My dad was deeply religious and wanted to raise us in the church, but things that should have been enjoyable—spending time with our cousins on Sabbath or singing worship songs with the family—became opportunities for abuse. The form of worship was there, but the spirit of Christian love was, too often, sadly absent.

CHAPTER EIGHT

"My mother worked too hard for me not to be great."
—Unknown

My brothers and I went to Christian private schools and eventually on to Christian universities. I was never sure how our parents afforded our tuition. One year my mom, who was always cooking and often had guests over for dinner, decided to cash in on her cooking skills. She had an idea to cook an Indian dinner and sell tickets for the event. The extra room in our house would fit a good number of tables to host the dinner, and the money raised would go toward our tuition.

My mom was very resourceful, but my dad always took things to the next level, often entering the realm of obnoxiousness. He instructed us to go through the church directory and call each family one by one, inform them about the Indian dinner at our house, which would serve as a fundraiser for our tuition. To close the deal, we were to ask how many tickets each family would like to purchase.

My dad wrote out the spiel he wanted us to recite and made us practice the delivery and intonation until we had his approval. He would then stand by while we made the calls. He was a master of manipulation and used our child voices to reel people in. How could people say no to little ones?

The plan was in full swing. My mom spent hours preparing, cooking, and cleaning for the mass of people. Her cooking was legendary. She cooked and they came. It was a success, and people donated money on top of their tickets. We hosted this dinner in Orlando at least twice. My dad had discovered a way to profit from his wife and children.

Moving to Orlando allowed my dad to continue working as a colporteur, when he chose to work. He knew how to turn on the charm when he wanted to. Sometimes I wondered if he really charmed people or if they just felt sorry for him. Whatever the case, he enjoyed his colporteuring work and we enjoyed one of its perks—the conferences, which were usually in a fun location and to which colporteurs' families were welcome.

These retreats were always exciting; the world as we knew it opened up a little wider. When I was in eighth grade, my dad took us with him to a conference at Daytona Beach. This was such a cool, happening spot! Going into the ocean, jumping waves, collecting shells, making castles in the sand—it was all so incredible. The shops on the boardwalk sold clothes that I had seen other girls wearing, but never in a million years would have thought of owning. After all, our family was poor enough that we hosted fundraisers to pay for our tuition; I would never have dreamed of asking for the extravagant clothes I saw in the shops along the boardwalk.

Yet as we passed the stores, I begged my parents to go into the ones that had name brand stuff that I was excited to simply be near. I saw the coolest pair of Jordache jeans! They had different Jordache designs on the pockets and they all had the horse that was the trademark on these crazy expensive jeans. I am not sure if my parents saw the drool coming out of my mouth, but I will never forget my dad's words: "Why don't you go try a pair on?"

I knew what we could afford and what we could not. I was not sure they had seen the price. My dad again asked me if I wanted to try them on. I didn't want to try them on and be disappointed, so I showed my parents the price tag, sure they would say no. But my mom said, "I know, go try them on if you like."

My jaw hung open as I looked for my size and tried on the jeans. They were supposed to be skin-tight but with my almost non-existent legs, they were loose enough not to horrify my parents. The commercial still echoes in my head as I recall the catchy tune—"You got the look…!"

I came out of the dressing room buzzing with pure joy. First of all, they fit! Second, I could not believe I was actually wearing them! Third, was it really possible that I might get them? The price tag was about $50! That was a fortune. I usually wore hand-me-downs, which was fine and just part of my reality. And when I did get new clothes, I was lucky to get jeans from Walmart for under $20.

I will never forget that moment. I have such clear memories of the stack of jeans, the dressing room, and the check out. I held my breath. I did not know how this was really happening! I felt such love from my parents, and I am sure it must have been so wonderful for them to make it possible.

As if that were not awesome enough, I was also gifted with my first pair of Nikes—$80 for a pair of shoes! They were a pair of Nike Cortez sneakers, with white leather and the red Nike swoosh. This was better than Christmas (which was typically a letdown). I hit the lottery on that trip. Going back to school, I felt so great. I was never one of the popular kids; I never had a bunch of friends. I was content with my two friends at school and my group of friends from church, but those Jordache jeans and Nike sneakers made me feel like I fit in. I felt such love and gratitude toward my parents for giving me some things that I wanted, despite our financial struggles.

CHAPTER NINE

"He who has not Christmas in his heart
will never find it under the tree."
—Roy L. Smith

The sounds of Salvation Army volunteers ringing bells and the sights of decorations and Christmas lights brightly shining ushered in the Christmas season. When I was a little girl, my family celebrated Christmas. As new immigrants, we didn't have a lot of money, but the smallest things put a smile on our faces. Spending time with our cousins who lived near us was always fun, as they were another set of brothers to us. There was food, family, and laughter. We did all the things that happy children did, chasing each other around the apartment, playing and fighting, laughing and crying, and Christmas just seemed so magical. I don't remember any of the gifts we received, but I know my mom found a way for us to have something special under the tacky Christmas tree that we just loved.

When we moved to Orlando, something triggered my dad to decide that Christmas was for heathens and therefore we would not celebrate this pagan holiday. Instead, we would celebrate the new year. New Year's Day, he asserted, was an occasion to celebrate. We would come together, make New Year's resolutions, and sometimes even get a present to welcome the new year.

I was heartbroken, but also annoyed that this was my dad's new thing. Why had it been OK for us to celebrate Christmas in years past? As a Christian, was there a better occasion to celebrate than Jesus's birth? I loved the magic of the Christmas story. Why did my dad think this was devilish now?

At our Christian school we were busy practicing for the Christmas program. My dad informed us that we would absolutely not celebrate Christmas, and we were not going to take part in the program. We were told that we needed to be an example to others. He instructed us to go to our teachers and let them know that we were not participating and why.

I loved my fifth-grade teacher. He was a kind man who I looked up to—the sort of man I wished my dad was. I wanted to be normal. I wanted to blend in. I wanted my dad to be like every other dad. Why did mine have to be so strange?

I went to my teacher, burning with embarrassment, and told him that we would not be attending the Christmas program. My teacher just assumed that we were going away or something and reassured me that it was not a problem. I was so happy to have a way out without having to disclose what I considered to be my dad's foolish reasoning.

The evening of the Christmas program came. To my shock, my dad told us to put our good clothes on. He announced that we were going to the school Christmas program—not to participate, but to enjoy the performance.

That day is burned indelibly in my memory. My mom protested, which antagonized my dad even more. "Stop undermining my authority!" he ordered.

We made our way to the auditorium and headed down the aisle to the front row. We sat front and center; he wanted us to be seen by all my classmates and teachers.

I refused to give in to tears; I did not want to give my dad the satisfaction of knowing that he was hurting me in such a profound way. I wasn't sure whether he was being cruel or crazy, but at that moment my heart began to shut my dad out.

During the three years we lived in Orlando, this became our way of life as far as Christmas went. My mom would sneak us a little gift, but the joy of Christmas that had been in my heart and that we once experienced began to fade with each passing year. My dad selfishly stole that Christmas spirit, something that to this day continues to leave a hole in my heart.

CHAPTER TEN

"Train up a child in the way he should go;
even when he is old he will not depart from it."
—Proverbs 22:6, ESV

My brothers and I had a very open relationship with my mom. There was not much we did not share with her. When I was in eighth grade, I had two girlfriends in my class that I was close to. One day at lunchtime, the topic of where babies came from was raised. My naivety was very obvious.

My friends giggled as they asked, "Don't you know where babies come from?"

Of course, I did! I mean, I was in eighth grade! With all the confidence in the world, I said, "From your stomach!"

I can still so clearly see us standing at the front of the classroom. They burst out laughing and laughed until they couldn't breathe! I just stood there, mortified. When they caught their breath, they shared with me where babies really came from.

I was horrified! I had seen the scars on my mom's belly. I knew that was where I had come from. How disgusting to think that babies would come from ... THERE!!!! My friends, still laughing, told me that I better go home and ask my mom about the facts of life.

I went home and told my mom what my friends had said. I revealed to her, with absolutely horror, where my friends thought babies came from. I will never forget my mom's face. She had the most sheepish, amused face as she tried hard not to giggle.

"Your friends are right," she confirmed. "That *is* where babies usually come from. But I had C-sections with you and both your brothers," she explained. Her children really *had* come from her belly.

I was both appalled and annoyed. Why hadn't she told me the truth about how babies were born long before I reached eighth grade? I felt like such a fool. She laughed, which of course infuriated me more.

"I was going to tell you," she said. "But I didn't think you needed to know yet."

My mom worked hard trying to balance home and work. She studied really hard to pass her boards. One of her teachers realized how much my mom was juggling and helped her study on the side. My mom sat for her nursing boards and passed with the highest marks in her class. She never received affirmation from anyone except her teacher, who declared to the whole class that my mom was a wife and a mother to three children, was working full-time, and had still passed with the highest grade.

My mom had friends, but during this period of her life they seemed to fade into the background. There was also underlying tension between my mom and my aunt, which my dad fueled by intentionally doing and saying things to create more friction between them. Years later, my aunt realized the truth and apologized to my mom, wishing she had seen past my dad's lies and manipulation.

Despite how annoyed I was when my mom set me straight about the facts of life, what I remember most now is the laughter I saw on her face that day. Looking back, I wish I had seen her look that way more often.

CHAPTER ELEVEN

"If it doesn't challenge you, it won't change you."
—Fred DeVito

In 1982, just after I graduated from eighth grade, our family moved yet again, this time to Dayton, Ohio. As an adult, when I asked my mom about why we moved to Ohio, she didn't have a real answer, except that my dad wanted to move.

I tried to imagine how his mind must have worked. Perhaps it was: "Hmmm, my wife and kids are happy here. They are active in church and school; they have great friends; and we have family here. Why stay? It's too normal. Where is the most random place we could go? I know—Ohio! Kettering has a church, a school, and a hospital affiliated with the church. It's perfect!"

I was heartbroken when we moved. I was a teenager, and change was hard. Life in Orlando had given me some security. I finally felt I had roots. But now I was leaving behind all I knew. Ohio, a place that was best known for IBM and Wright Patterson Air Force Base, sounded very boring. How could Dayton, Ohio compare to sunshine, beaches, Disney, friends, and my life as I knew it?

From day one, life in this new place was very stressful. The school was predominantly white, and it appeared that everyone came from affluent homes. Even the few minorities at the school seemed to be from wealthy families. My first day of school was an excruciating experience of not belonging and being spoken to by only a handful of people.

School remained a very isolating, lonely place. If I could have had a superpower, it would have been to make myself invisible. Not everyone was horrible, yet the few kids with ugly attitudes seemed large and overpowering. They seemed to be everywhere and when in their presence, I tried unsuccessfully to shrink. I never felt welcomed, or like I was a part of any social circles. I wanted so badly to be part of the "normal" world that others enjoyed. But a huge part of me was also afraid of letting anyone get too close. I didn't want others to know the reality of my life.

We rented a house just a few minutes from the school. Our house was the only part of that move that felt OK to me, as it was a nice change from the apartments we had lived in. I had my own room and often escaped there, crying and begging God to do something. I am not sure what I expected, but when I look back now, I realize that the "thing" God did do was equip me with strength to live the life I had been given.

My dad told us that God did not want us to have worldly things, which included buying a house. He told us that God was building a heavenly home for us so there was no need for one here on earth, which is why we always rented our housing. But during our second year in Dayton, my parents bought a house. I never asked what led to this decision; I was just happy that we finally had a home.

I hoped this meant we would not have to move again. In our nine years in Toronto we had lived in seven different apartments; in three years in Orlando we had lived in four different places. When my folks bought the house in Dayton, I hoped it would change the pattern of constantly packing and unpacking. Obviously, my mom did 99 percent of the packing, cleaning, and unpacking all those times. Looking back on all this as an adult, I wonder how she did this while working full time, cooking, and taking care of us.

Though I was happy we were buying a home, my brothers and I wished we could have stayed in the lower middle-class neighborhood where our rented house was located. Our new house, which we never saw until we moved in, was on the last street that was considered zoned in the city. It was the nicest house on the street, but that wasn't saying much. Driving down the street for the first time, we passed family homes with picket fences that may have been cute at one time. Now these houses struggled to stay upright, the white siding faded, the screen doors hanging unsteadily on the door frame, just waiting for the inevitable fall onto steps that themselves were weary and cracked with age. The yards were parched from dehydration. The picket fences, no longer white, were now gap-toothed with missing pieces and rotted wood that showed its age. Many of the structures bore no resemblance to what they had been in their former glory. Most of the homes were in similar condition, at varying stages of dilapidation. We continued silently down the pebbled road, inhaling our new neighborhood, unable to exhale.

My dad drove to the end of the street. Directly in front of us was a levee—a hill we could easily climb—beside a bike path that followed a river. To the left of us was a train overpass. The neighbors directly across from us seemed to have a bit more property, but their home was a shack with no washroom or running water. In this neighbor's yard were a few scary dogs, a water pump, an outhouse, and a few disheveled children who seemed to be our age, two boys and a girl. I wondered what twilight zone we had entered. To the right of the road sat our new-to-us home, the first house my parents ever owned. It was a three-bedroom brick bungalow. Compared to the neighbors, we lived in a dream house.

We had a pebble driveway, with a garage that could be used for storage. The inside of the house was pretty normal. The front door opened directly into a large living room; beyond that was a hallway with a bathroom and three bedrooms, and on the other side of the house, a dining room and kitchen. It was a simple layout with potential. The backyard was quite large, and my dad made use of it by planting a huge garden with all sorts of plants and veggies. Behind us was a trailer park.

That calm we enjoyed in this new house was short-lived. The incident that shattered this period of calm started, as my dad's outbursts so often did, in the car.

My mom had finished working the 11:00 p.m.–7:00 a.m. shift, and we had picked her up from the hospital on our way to school. We stopped at a full-service gas station for fuel. My brothers and I were otherwise engaged until my dad's tone penetrated our banter and caused familiar shivers to wash over us. While we weren't paying close attention to what he was actually saying, we could hear his voice become louder and louder as he enunciated each word.

In response to whatever my dad must have said, my mom retorted, "Why don't *you* go get a job?" She must have known this comment would end with him beating her. He began to yell, "You think you are better than me because you have an education?!" He grabbed her hair and pulled her head toward him. With the other hand he pounded the back of her neck. We were shocked. We had never seen our dad physically hurt our mom to this degree. We yelled at him to stop, but he didn't stop until he noticed the gas station attendant watching. Then he released my mom and said, "Let's go home. I am going to kill you."

He drove us to school. My brothers and I jumped out of our vehicle, grabbing backpacks and trying to shake off the nerves as we gave my mom a hug, hating to leave her. Would he really kill her? As I hugged my mom, she whispered into my ear, "If anything happens to me, take your brothers and go to Auntie S's house."

As I watched my parents drive away from the school and turn right toward home, I felt sick to my stomach. Would this be the last time I hugged my mom? How did she think it was possible that I could take my brothers to Maryland, where her family lived? It was more than 400 miles away, an eight-hour drive.

It was an agonizing morning at school. I had no one to turn to. Even if the teachers had been more approachable, how could I go up to one of them and say, "I'm worried my dad is killing my mom right now"? I only had God, so I prayed literally all morning. I begged Him to please keep my mom alive. I begged Him to please protect us and, if something did happen, to help me find a way to get to my aunt's home.

Remembering those hours even now, so many years later, my heart still pounds and an indescribable anxiety still fills me. My brothers were twelve and nine. I had just turned fourteen. I sat in my classes, petrified. I went to the washroom and stood in the middle stall, after looking under the other two stalls to make sure they were empty. With tears rolling down my cheeks, I wondered how I was going to survive the next hours. How was I going to keep my brothers safe?

I had to know if my dad had killed her. I had to have a plan. I went to the payphone on the wall by the boys' washroom. The office was right across from me. I stood on the carpet that was stained from the thousands of little feet that had run over those threads. I held the phone in my shaking hands, wondering what I would do if HE answered? I did not have the needed quarter to make the call, so I had to call collect. I pressed 0 for the operator, telling her I wanted to make "a collect call from Reema." I recited the seven numbers and then waited, holding my breath, having no clue what I would do if my dad answered.

The operator dialed the number. I heard my mom answer, laughingly, "Hello, yes. I'll accept the call." I was furious!

"I'm calling to see if you're OK," I told her, my voice shaking.

"I'm fine, there's nothing to worry about," she told me, her tone light and happy, as if nothing was wrong.

Years later, I shared with my mom what living through that morning was like and how it continued to affect me. I cried myself to sleep for many a night, truly having only God to turn to. Protecting my little brothers was just a given, but that day, for the first time in my life I understood with certainty that my mom was my responsibility too.

Today, if there is any suspicion of abuse, school officials are bound by law to report it to the authorities. I am baffled that so many people turned their heads and ignored what was happening in our home. There were friends who knew. There were teachers who knew—or at least suspected. Why did no one approach my mom? Our principal knew. I told him as much, at least twice.

With our family life being what it was, it was no surprise that my siblings and I had anger issues. This was especially true of Kumar, and it didn't take much to set him off at school. Kumar had a strong dislike of others touching his food. One day his class was in the cafeteria, some ordering hot lunches and others eating their lunches from home. It was broccoli cheese soup day, an absolute favorite of ours. We saw it as such a treat to order from the cafeteria. Someone reached across the table to grab something on Kumar's tray. Kumar warned the other child: "Don't touch my food."

The child took another piece of Kumar's lunch. My brother, in an unwitting reflection of my dad's temper, yelled, "I TOLD YOU NOT TO TOUCH MY FOOD!!!" He then took his tray of food—soup and all— hurled it against the cafeteria wall and walked out.

I heard about this from Kumar when he informed me that he had a two-day suspension. The principal explained that he understood

Kumar's anger, but his behavior was not acceptable.

This was on the cusp of one of my dad's volatile explosions. I was so scared of what would happen to Kumar if my dad learned of his behavior. I was in 10th grade and, being the invisible girl, I had never set foot in the principal's office. Yet I felt I had no choice but to approach the man.

I went into the principal's office, stared at him seated on the other side of his desk and wrung my shaking hands. I begged him to allow Kumar to do an in-school suspension, because if my dad found out, we would be in for it. He agreed. I am not sure what he knew, but he must have realized that life was horrible for us. Why else would a 10th grader come into his office begging for her brother to have an in-school suspension?

After my dad threatened to kill my mom, my uncle called the principal and asked to speak with me. My uncle knew the principal well; they had worked together in a previous school. I was called to the office and spoke to my uncle, who asked if we were OK. The principal must have known that all was not well in our home. Other people also knew this, yet no one did anything to help us.

CHAPTER TWELVE

"Don't be afraid of being different. Be afraid of being the same."
—Unknown

My dad had many eccentric interests and behaviors. Some of these were likely symptoms of mental illness; others were relatively harmless quirks that, in a different person, might even have been amusing or endearing. But in every case, his obsessions led to anger and usually violence when his wife and children violated any of his unwritten rules.

While we were taught not to focus on worldly possessions, my dad had a fixation with certain things. We did not have much money, yet we had a 60-inch television in our home. It was not just a TV, but a

TV with a built-in phone system. I didn't know anyone else who had something like this in late 80s. In the living/dining/kitchen area, we had at least six phones. We didn't actually have an ordinary phone, only novelty phones in the shape of some object or character. There was the one built into the TV, a Snoopy phone, a Mickey Mouse phone, an old-fashioned phone, a piano phone, and a race car phone.

Then there was my dad's fixation with flashlights—not the everyday kind, but the foot-long, heavy duty Maglites that required six D batteries. The batteries cost more than the flashlights! Pens were another obsession. He always carried a four-color BIC pen that we were never allowed to touch. Of course, this made us want to use it all the more.

At one point, he became intrigued with budgies. Instead of buying a normal bird cage and a couple of birds, my dad had a cage built, from floor to ceiling, approximately 3 ft. in diameter. He filled the cage with more than a dozen budgies. The house was no longer a quiet place. The chirping was incessant. And as with everything else, my dad never dirtied his own hands, but left it to my mom to clean the cage.

Leaving others to do his work was one of my dad's defining traits, and he was often very creative at figuring out ways to do this. Route 48 was a main road in Dayton that went right downtown, intersecting with Third Street, one of the busiest spots in the city. Everyone seemed to pass this intersection during business hours. My dad had the bright idea of selling magazines to these commuters as they rushed to catch the bus or headed home after a busy day. He acquired a large stock of religious magazines from our denomination, which he planned to sell for $1 each.

The clincher was that he was not going to be selling the magazines himself. No, his children would do the selling. I was fifteen at the time, and to me, summer meant sleeping in, reading, and just hanging out, not carrying out a horribly embarrassing idea that my eccentric dad drummed up.

To add to the humiliation, my dad had someone make these apron-like garments for us to wear. The aprons went over our head and had big pockets at the front and back where we could stash the magazines and keep them organized. There was also a smaller pocket to hold the cash. It was *not* a garment a teenage girl wanted to be seen wearing at the busiest intersection in town!

My dad would drive us downtown, set us up at the corner of Route 48 and Third Street, and leave us there for hours in the summer heat. This was long before the era of cell phones, so we had no way of reaching him if we needed to.

I begged my mom to make him end the nightmare. I asked if I could work at the greenhouse at the school instead. Some girls in my class worked there, and it seemed like fun and a good way to make friends as well as some money. My dad flatly said no. No reason, just "I said no!"

I was mortified as we carried out his ridiculous mission. To make matters worse, I realized, to my dismay, that the magazines we were selling for $1 were outdated! These were cast-offs the church was getting rid of, so the profit margin was 100 percent! Unfortunately, the embarrassment factor was also 100 percent. My dad gave us a script to use, though after a bit, we gave up on the script and just asked passers-by, "Would you like to buy a magazine?" We left out the part my dad wanted us to add: "The money is for our tuition."

People would see our pathetic faces and give us money out of pure pity, often telling us to keep the magazine ... or the change ... or both. Basically, we were beggars. This memory still makes me want to cry for that younger me.

There were also repercussions at the end of the day if we had not sold all our magazines. Kumar always sold the most; he was the youngest and the cutest, which seemed to factor into his success. We quickly learned to share the money amongst ourselves and throw out magazines so the number of magazines matched our dollars. Looking back as adults, we still cringe when we think of those aprons and shudder at the thought of enduring that summer.

Our lives became much more volatile around this time. What changed or triggered my dad, I am not sure. We were, as I've said, a very religious family on the outside. We sat in the second row from the front at church, and we were always on time or my dad would have a fit. He drilled into us, "If you are late here on earth, you will be late for heaven."

My mom began to take more Saturday shifts at work. I believe she did this so she would not have to go to church and deal with my dad. After church we would head across the street to the hospital and have lunch with my mom in the cafeteria. Her face would light up at seeing us, but she couldn't fully hide the conflicting emotions that played across her face when she saw my dad.

One Sabbath, when my mom did have the day off, we came home from church to a beautiful meal she had cooked for us. The table was set and we all took our places.

Among my dad's many idiosyncrasies was the fact that he did not like to eat with a fork. He did not like a teaspoon or tablespoon either. We had an in-between sized spoon, which was his.

The food was on the table. My dad sat down, then realized he had been given an ordinary spoon to eat with rather than his "special" spoon. Something in him snapped. He stood up, with his voice escalating in volume, enunciating each word. "How many times have I told you that I do not want this spoon? How many times must I say it?!!"

With one hand, he swept all the food off the table. Plates broke, food splashed and spilled everywhere. Before he could become even more physically violent, my mom ushered us out the door. She did not drive, so we all went and sat on the levee. A short time earlier, our stomachs had been rumbling, but hunger was now secondary to the numbing fear we each felt. We were grateful to be out of the house and away from my dad.

After we'd been outside for about an hour and a half, my mom led us back into the house. My dad was sitting on a chair in the living room as if nothing had happened. The mess in the kitchen, however, was just as we'd left it an hour and a half before. It would have been unimaginable to think that he might clean it up. We scurried around on our hands and knees, picking up shards of glass, and soaking up and wiping down the mess of food spilled everywhere.

My dad never apologized. He pretended nothing had happened, and my mom followed his lead and also pretended the same. We children found this confusing, but not out of the ordinary. It was how our family usually dealt with my dad's outbursts.

Gardening was one of my dad's passions. He did not have a normal sized garden plot, but a huge one that required constant attention. He forced me and my siblings to weed the garden at the crack of dawn. As teenagers, being awakened at that ungodly hour felt like cruel and unusual punishment.

My dad was certain that cow manure was the best fertilizer for his precious garden. The garden store sold various kinds of manure in bags, but my dad wanted us to experience the thrill of getting our hands dirty. He found a farm where manure was free for the taking as long as we helped ourselves. The stench of simply picking up dog poop is distasteful enough. Being in the middle of cow dung, with the stench embedding itself into our pores, was horrendous! "Appalled" is too mild a word to express how we felt. We were city kids! My dad, of course, did not lift a finger or get his hands dirty as we gathered the stinking piles of cow manure for his garden.

Another of his eccentricities involved the source of our drinking water. Down the road from our home was a nuclear plant. This plant was most famous during WWII for its nuclear operations. During the time that we lived there, the plant had discontinued the detonator work, but it continued to make nuclear power generators. We wondered what other secretive things occurred there.

Up to that point, we had always lived in the city and drank water from the tap. Once we moved to the outskirts of Dayton, my dad decided, partly because of the nearby nuclear plant, that the water did not taste right. So, he found another way to get us water. We didn't have the extra money for things like a water cooler or bottled water, but someone told my dad of a spring flowing down a little hill near one of the country roads. It was supposedly great drinking water and had other health benefits too. My dad was always ready to try something new, especially since he could rely on my mom to clean up his messes.

My dad would load forty or fifty recycled milk jugs in our van. We would make the scenic drive to the spring and fill our water jugs. One by one, jug by jug, with lids screwed on one after another. We did this week after week.

For some reason, probably the change of seasons, we stopped using the spring as our main water source. But my dad had mastered the art of getting the most for the least. He went to our school and delivered a sob story about us not being able to have drinking water and asked if we could fill up at the school. The custodian, a lovely man, likely saw no harm in allowing my dad to access the water at the school. I wish I could have seen this kind man's face when my dad had us bring in our jugs, ten by ten by ten by ten, until they were all there. We filled them all from the sink in the boys' bathroom. We did this every weekend. The sweet custodian was there every weekend; he often left the door open for us to access the bathroom. How kind he was to us. He treated us as if this was a normal occurrence. People like that custodian probably never realized what an impact their kindness had on us.

My dad's beliefs changed according to what served him best. In our very strict Christian household, going to the movies was not something we did. We were led to believe that the movie theater was a godless place; we watched the same movies that were in theaters at home, just a few months later. This was frustrating, as my classmates were allowed to go to movies and I often heard them talking about the latest film that I knew nothing about.

When the movie *Gandhi* came out, it was a big deal for my parents. There was pride and curiosity about this film, given our Indian heritage, so my parents decided that we would go to the theater to see *Gandhi*. It was finally happening! We were going to the theatre to see a movie! My parents would see that it was a safe place to be, and we could finally do something every other normal kid enjoyed.

I don't really remember a lot about *Gandhi*, aside from the basics. My dad told us a lot about Gandhi and the Indian independence movement and how the events of that time had impacted his family. I was simply happy to be attending a movie in a theatre. Then came the harsh verdict: despite having seen *Gandhi*, we were still not allowed to go to the movies! There was no logical reason. It was simply another one of those, "Because I said so" reasons.

My dad's violence could be triggered by the most random things. Once, Kumar was using the bathroom and as he put the toilet seat lid down, it slipped from his hand, slamming the lid. My dad came racing out of the kitchen, grabbed my shocked brother, and pulled him back into the bathroom, yelling, "How many times have I told you not to drop the toilet seat lid? I AM GOING TO TEACH YOU TO NEVER DO THAT AGAIN!!!"

With this, he locked the door and began beating my brother. We could hear Kumar crying while apologizing and promising, "I'll never do it again!" My dad kept beating him.

Outside the door, my mom begged my dad to stop and to beat her instead. She told me to go get a butter knife, which she used to pry the lock so the door would open. Hearing her picking at the lock, my dad shouted, "IF YOU COME IN, I WILL KILL YOU!!!"

My mom opened the door. My dad released Kumar and grabbed my mom's hair, pulling her toward him. From somewhere he grabbed a two-by-four and began beating her thigh. Over and over he whacked her, yelling some gibberish and belittling her.

Certain that he was going to kill her, I ran and called 911, begging them to help. "My dad is beating my mom! He's trying to kill her!!" I blubbered into phone.

By the time the police came, my dad had stopped. The purple blotches stood out vividly even on my mom's dark skin. The police took their statements. My dad turned on the charm, as he could do when he wanted to. By the time the police officer had finished taking their statements, he was sitting at the table sympathizing with my dad. They were sharing stories of the woes of dealing with their wives.

The police did not write my dad up. In later years that cop and my dad would wave as they passed each other on the road. I learned then that the police were not there to help; they could not see the truth even when the black and blue was right in front of their faces.

Chapter Thirteen

"Stop sitting in the passenger seat of your life. Take the wheel!"
—Srishti Bhayana

Though our family life continued to be volatile, the stability of owning a home felt good. My dad gave up colporteuring and took a job in the hospital's transportation department—though, of course, he ended up quitting that job before long. My mom encouraged him to take classes in business, which seemed to give him some purpose and boost his confidence. But when he received his diploma, that was the end of that. He continued to disappear most of the day, leaving us unsure of what he did or where he went, and leaving my mother with the burden of supporting our family.

My mom worked constantly, with shifts that were often back to back. Not having a driver's license, she was dependent on my dad for transportation. My dad knew that he was my mom's ride and yet sometimes he simply did not pick her up. She would have to walk the nine miles home, exhausted, with no funds for a cab, as my dad also controlled our family's money.

The fact that my dad was the sole driver in the family also meant that he could use the car to exert control over us. Sometimes he controlled us by refusing to drive us where we wanted to go. On one occasion, my class was having a party at a classmate's home. The event was supervised and school approved; everyone was going. I asked if I could go. My dad said, "Sure!" And then, before I could get too excited, he added, "As long as you have a ride."

Did I mention that we lived on the edge of town, one street away from the city limits? We were too far out of the way for anyone to offer me a ride, assuming there was someone I could have asked. Why would he do this? How hard was it to drive me the fifteen or twenty minutes to the party? And why did he appear to derive such pleasure from making me unhappy? It was just another way he exerted control over me.

Most siblings fight over the front seat of a vehicle, and in our younger years my brothers and I were no exception. "I get the front seat!" Then the inevitable, "You had it last time!" This was a common argument that occurred over the years, until one day it came to an abrupt halt.

My mom was at work. My dad had taken us with him to run an errand, and Kumar had won the front seat. My dad got lost and he asked Kumar to call out to a man who was approaching us so he could ask for directions. Kumar called out, using his index finger to beckon the man.

After receiving directions and thanking the man, my dad angrily rolled up the window. He was furious that Kumar had beckoned the man with his index finger. "That is how you call dogs!!" he screamed. "You use four fingers to call a human being!"

He began hitting my brother, banging Kumar's head repeatedly against the glass window beside him. I cautiously slipped my sweater along the window to try to soften the impact of those blows.

That was the last time we fought over the "privilege" of sitting in the front seat. From then on, we fought quietly amongst ourselves over which unfortunate sibling would be obligated to sit in the front seat next to our dad.

Fear controlled my existence. I was an obedient child, but my obedience was grounded in fear, not respect. If told not to, I did not. The risk of being caught was never worth breaking the rules.

After I earned my driver's license, I became the second driver in the family. I drove myself and my brothers to school and back every day. The car radio was always tuned to the same Christian radio station that woke us up every day at 6:00 a.m.—"WFCJ: The Sound of the New Life." It was the only radio station we were allowed to listen to.

We had been taught that rock and roll was of the devil. Fear kept us from changing the radio dial, even when it was just me and my two brothers in the car. Then one day, Rajiv waited until we were at the end of the street and turned the dial to 99.9 FM, the Top 40 station. This was the station that played everyday songs that every other teenager knew: Michael Jackson, Prince, Billy Joel, and more.

I stared at him. "Are you crazy? Dad will kill us!"

"He'll never know. We'll change it back to WFCJ before we get home."

Though rationally I knew Rajiv was right and our dad would not find out, I was petrified. I was sure my dad knew what we were doing even when he wasn't in the vehicle with us. Still, this became our routine from that point on. At seventeen years old, I was finally listening to music I wanted to hear. We never got caught. And at some point we just transitioned to listening to hit songs on our Walkman's while we traveled with our parents.

As a teen, I wanted to experience some social freedom. I would ask to go to the mall to meet my one friend. I was a really good kid. I never gave my parents cause to question my behavior; I was just asking to walk around the mall with my girlfriend as any teenager might do. And since I could now drive myself around, it wasn't even an inconvenience to my parents. Instead of a simple yes or no, my dad would grant his permission, but only if I took Rajiv with me.

There was no rhyme or reason to this stipulation. I was already driving everywhere my parents needed me to go, often alone. When we needed milk, I went; when my mom had an appointment, I drove. I was always doing the little errands that required a vehicle, which freed my dad up. Driving to the mall to hang out with my friend for a couple of hours was a simple request. Telling me that I had to take my younger brother along just felt spiteful. And Rajiv didn't even want to go!

My mom had always wanted to learn how to drive, but over the years, my dad used this as a means of further deriding and breaking her down. Whenever he took her out for a driving lesson he gave her no encouragement, only criticism. It was daunting enough that she was trying to learn how to drive in a twelve-passenger Ford Econoline— not the ideal vehicle for a beginner. But whenever she was behind the wheel, my dad would not shut up for a minute. "You're going to the left too much!" or "You're weaving!" or "You're going too slow!!" he would snap. My mom was already scared of her own shadow whenever she sat behind the wheel, and my dad refused to create a safe atmosphere that encouraged her success. If I hadn't taken driver's education classes, I probably would never have received my license either.

At the age of fifty, my mom finally took driving lessons and received her license. She loved the freedom it gave her. But a few years later, she realized that she needed to give up driving, for her safety as well as the safety of others. She was so belittled and broken down by my dad that she could not function without being consumed by fear.

By this time, I was beginning to hate my dad. I sometimes wished he would die, not because I wished him pain but because it seemed like the only way out for us. I wanted him to disappear; his presence in our lives only brought embarrassment, pain, and disappointment. I never understood why my mom married him or why she stayed. I realized that he was necessary for my existence, but his purpose had already been served. He had no reason to be in our lives.

There had been moments when I felt hopeful, perhaps when I saw my parents hold hands while walking somewhere. My brothers and I would glance at each other, cautiously optimistic that this was the start of happiness. Eventually that hope evaporated. I learned to be grateful for the moments that resembled what I imagined to be a normal family life.

During our teen years, Kumar was obsessed with Oprah Winfrey and her show. We often watched the show together, intrigued by her guests. In one particular episode, Oprah's guests were women whose husbands beat them. She called them "Battered Women." Kumar and I looked at each other. We didn't speak, yet plenty was said.

A battered woman. For the first time we realized there was a name for this and my mom was not the only one. Apparently this happened to women of all races and economic status. It was horrible, and like our mother, it seemed as though many women stayed with their abuser. In that particular episode, Oprah was helping those women leave their ugly situations, showing them that there was hope.

For the first time I believed there was the possibility for change. There *was* hope. My mom could have a life where she, and in turn, we, did not have to live in fear of beatings and violence.

CHAPTER FOURTEEN

"Happiness is not by chance but by choice."
—Jim Rohn

Despite my dad's treatment of my mom, she always went out of her way to bless him with things she knew he would enjoy. She learned to cook food from his part of India. Most days she made two separate meals, as she did not really enjoy the same food that he did, but she was willing to put forth the extra effort to make him happy.

When his fiftieth birthday arrived, she planned a party for him. Everyone was excited! My mom bought my dad the best present, one that he could not have imagined. I have a picture of this moment in my mind's eye. I see myself waiting in eager anticipation, with my bobbed haircut, my huge thick glasses that dwarfed my face, my wide grin with crooked teeth, watching as my dad opened his present. My mom stood off to the side, smiling. She looked so beautiful as she watched my dad, and she must have known he would behave this time, since we had people over.

My dad unwrapped the gift, taking out the coolest video camera! It was a large, professional camera that sat on your shoulder, like the ones TV newscasters used.

That camera became my dad's security blanket; it went everywhere with him. It was like an extension of his body, as he videoed everything. Eventually, videotaping was not enough. He learned how to make countless copies of these videos and would give them to people, never asking if they wanted the videos or not. It also became another way to embarrass his children as he directed us, telling us where to stand or how to pose.

In contrast, my dad never gave my mom a gift of any kind, unless you consider a life with post-traumatic stress disorder to be a gift. She lived in a constant state of fear. Unless we called out to her as we approached, she would always react with fear, a gasp that was always accompanied with her hands flying up in front of her face in a defensive position. She reacted in this way for the rest of her life, until she took her last breath.

Most of my memories of my mom are of her in constant motion. On the rare occasions when she wasn't cooking, cleaning, or working outside the house, she loved reading romance novels. My dad hated her reading, so she would read while my dad was not at home. As soon as she heard the car pulling up on the gravel, she'd stash her book and pretend she was doing something else. He controlled her with constant fear and seemed to hate anything that gave her the smallest pleasure.

As a child, I saw my mother as a quiet lady who was always behind the scenes, but in retrospect, I can see that she was actually a social person. She wanted to disappear when my dad was around, but there was a reason for that. He had to be the center of attention and constantly found ways to belittle her. When we had family friends over for meals and socializing, the men would congregate in one spot and the women elsewhere, usually in the kitchen. In this setting, away from my dad, my mom seemed to come out of her shell, laughing and enjoying herself.

My mom had some friendships at work, but nothing that allowed her to share deeply. Her friends stayed in touch, but usually called her when my dad was not home. Some of her friends were in marriages where, while there was no physical abuse, there was definitely emotional abuse. With some of these friends, the women found solace in each other.

But her children remained the most important people in her life. Looking at this season of my mom's life, it was easy to see another reason we were her everything. She loved hearing our stories and she did as best she could under the circumstances to provide us with a "normal" life.

Many of my parents' friends were former classmates from India. There was an immediate bond between our families. "Stranger Danger" was something my siblings and I had heard about, especially with my mom working at the hospital. But we were never taught that the danger could come from family and friends.

One particular family came over more than others, I think because my dad connected with the husband. On one visit, my mom and "aunt" (every familiar adult is an aunt or uncle in Indian culture) were busy cooking in the kitchen. This couple had a son and baby daughter; the son was playing with my brothers, while I was lucky enough to hold the baby. I loved babies!

My "uncle" was fiddling with my mom's sewing machine to see if he could get it going for her. He called me into the room and asked me if I could thread the needle, as he could not see well enough. The door was open and looked right into the living room. I sat on the edge of the bed, holding his baby girl, listening to his instructions.

Suddenly I felt his hands slipping under my shirt, fondling my developing breast. I was holding his daughter on my lap. I froze! This was an "uncle" who had always treated me lovingly, and I adored him. What was he doing? And why?

I'm sure God nudged my mom into calling me for something. I was so grateful and couldn't pass the baby to him fast enough as I ran out of there. His wife was in the kitchen, right around the corner from where he violated my trust.

He never said anything, and yet when we saw each other the few times after that, he always gave me a look that creeped me out. Years later, he still gave me that creepy smile, as if we shared a secret. I told my mom a few weeks later. I know she told my dad, but he never said anything to me about it. Not long after this, the family moved to another state and I was relieved not to have to see this "uncle" anymore.

CHAPTER FIFTEEN

"The weak can never forgive.
Forgiveness is the attribute of the strong."
—Mahatma Gandhi

From the time I was a very young child I believed in God's miraculous powers. He parted the waters for Moses. He caused a blind man to see. He even raised Lazarus from the dead. So I knew He could definitely heal my dad from whatever possessed him.

After a beating, I would earnestly pray for God to please change my dad into a kind and loving father. I often prayed that my mom would leave my dad. This was a prayer I had prayed since I was little. These prayers kept hope alive.

As I entered high school I realized that those prayers were not going to be answered. I understood that my dad had to want help in order to change, to better himself. Unfortunately, he was, by definition, a narcissist. In his view, we were the problem. If we would just listen, he would not have to beat us.

Instead, God answered my prayers in a totally different way. He gave me strength to endure and to survive.

I loved God with all my heart. I wanted so badly to be baptized. I was ready. I was eager to make this commitment, just as I had been taught I should from a young age. From the age of thirteen, I took baptismal courses through the mail and completed them a few times. I had wanted to get baptized with my friends while we lived in Florida. But every time I asked, my dad told me I was not ready. Frustrated, I wondered how *he* could know if I was ready or not.

My sixteenth birthday, which was also my brother Rajiv's fourteenth birthday, fell on Sunday, September 23, 1984. My dad announced with excitement that all three of us would be getting baptized on the Sabbath before our birthday. It would be a celebration, and what could be better than giving our hearts to the Lord on His day?

I was so upset. I had been forced to wait until I was sixteen years old for my dad to agree that I was ready to be baptized, yet my brothers, ages fourteen and eleven, were suddenly old enough just because he wanted to stage this event on our birthday weekend? It was unfair. I hated his controlling nature.

Although I had already studied for baptism, my dad had all of us take baptismal classes with the youth pastor. He seemed very excited about our baptism, which should have been a huge clue that he was planning something.

Unbeknownst to us, the mission field that the church was focusing on at that particular time happened to be India. When the day came for our baptism, my dad had planned the whole service. He was leading the adult Sabbath School (known in other churches as Sunday School) and he had the music, mission stories, and the whole program planned.

My dad had my mom with him in front of the large congregation that day, reading from his notes about the missions in India. My mom sometimes reminded me of Princess Diana. Princess Di had that shy look when she was in the spotlight, especially in her early days. My mom, standing up front with my dad while he led the song service, had that same look as they sang the hymns. I have never heard my mom sing for anyone except my children. I can only imagine that she probably wished the church floor would swallow her up.

This church in our community was probably 90 percent white, predominantly upper class, well-educated folks. My family fell into the .02 percent category—poor, minority, and weird. At least, my dad was so weird that we were easily overshadowed with him in the spotlight. He really had no shame; nothing embarrassed him. This day that was supposed to be a celebration of our decision to follow Christ was really all about him.

As I headed into the sanctuary, I noticed women from the church wearing saris. I was confused, then embarrassed, and finally mortified when I realized that my dad had asked the women to wear saris. My poor, shy mom had to coordinate this for at least twenty women.

When Sabbath School ended, I was grateful the foolishness was over. The members of the church had been educated about India and the needs of the church there. Money was collected and my dad was very pleased. It was all over and church, I thought, would be normal. We would be baptised during the service: my parents would come forward, we would be immersed in water, and the pastor would pray over us. What could possibly go wrong?

Maybe that was the problem right there. I figured there was nothing more that could embarrass me—that after turning the spotlight on himself during Sabbath School, my dad would retreat to some semblance of a normal person during the baptism itself.

My brothers and I were in the baptismal tank. The pastor asked my parents, family, and friends to come forward. I saw my mom coming forward. I knew she was very proud of us, but the look on her face didn't make sense. Other people who were part of our lives were coming forward, but I didn't see my dad.

Then I saw a man walking down the aisle toward the baptismal tank, wearing a turban. Who could that possibly be? Sikhs were the ones who wore the turban as part of their religious dress, and we had no Sikhs in our circle of friends. As this turban wearing man raised his head, I saw that it was my dad, proudly wearing a large, heavily ornate turban.

I had often been grateful that blushing was not something obviously visible on my face due to my skin tone. But in that moment, nothing could hide the severe reddening of my face, ears, and neck as blood coursed through my whole body with heat escaping through my pores as if I had a 104 F fever. How was this possible? What would make this man who I had to call my dad do such an idiotic thing? How was I to ever show my face again? Not even being immersed in baptism could wash away the mortification of that moment.

After the service, there was an Indian themed luncheon, made by my mom, that served between sixty and seventy people. How my mom managed all this, I never knew. There would have been the shopping, prepping, cooking, packaging, and transporting of all the food, along with the serving and cleaning.

As was typical, my dad didn't think to thank my mom for her hard work. Instead, he found ways to take credit for all the things she labored over. "If you like the food, tell me, if you don't, tell my wife," he would still say. And he would get the laughs he was looking for every time, even if some of them were uncomfortable laughs. My mom had a strong and quiet faith, and I am sure it is only by God's grace that she endured all that she did.

CHAPTER SIXTEEN

"When we give cheerfully and accept gratefully,
everyone is blessed."
—Maya Angelou

As I mentioned earlier, my dad ruined Christmas when we were children, and we were no longer allowed to celebrate it. This changed again several years after we moved to Ohio. My folks opened a seniors' home, and after that "Traditional Christmas" was back—at least, in appearance. We had the obligatory tacky Christmas tree with dollar store ornaments. There were little presents for the seniors who lived there. And, as she had always done, my mom tried her best to buy us little gifts to make our Christmas special.

As my brothers and I grew older and earned money with our part-time jobs, we began to buy gifts ourselves. We always tried to buy my mom something that she would like, but, ironically, we put the most thought and consideration into finding a gift for my dad.

At some point, before we awoke on Christmas morning, my dad would disappear without warning, stealing Christmas again with his absence. We never knew where he went or what he did. He always showed up in the evening, and we all acted as if nothing were amiss. We would present him with our gifts, the ones that we had spent so much time and effort on, hoping we got it right. Looking back, I now understand that we worked the hardest on my dad's gifts because we were desperately seeking his love and appreciation.

On one particular Christmas night when we were all in our teens, my dad had come home from his Christmas hiding spot and was sitting in the living room. My brothers and I presented him with the gift we had chosen for him. Kumar handed it to him and my dad replied, "Thank you very much." The gift sat on his lap unopened. He did not touch it.

I wanted to yell at him to open the present that we had taken so much time, energy, and thought to give him—not to mention the money we'd spent. I wanted to scream, demanding that he appreciate it. But what I really wanted was to beg him to simply love us and appreciate our gesture. We were past expecting gifts from him. We were past hoping for Christmases like normal people. We didn't even expect him to be at the table for Christmas dinner. Was it too much to ask him to OPEN THE GIFT WE BOUGHT HIM?

I wish I could have read his mind at that moment. Was he uncomfortable, or sad, or embarrassed?

Kumar took the gift, held it over his lap and opened it for him. When our dad still failed to respond, Kumar even reacted on his behalf: "Oh wow, it's a watch!"

At that moment, something snapped inside me. It was as if my emotions had been disconnected, or perhaps as if a protective wall had been erected around my heart. My dad was one of the few people who had the power to really hurt me. He had continued to hurt me over the years, but that Christmas night, as I watched him ignore the present we had chosen for him with such care, I realized that my heart's desire was never going to come to fruition. This man, who professed to be a man of God, had completely missed God's command to love and take care of his family. After that Christmas, I stopped expecting anything from my dad.

Our community was a cliquish one, where everyone seemed to be someone. In my school and church community, most kids came from families of doctors, lawyers, teachers, or pastors. From my perspective as a teenager, it seemed that even those who weren't wealthy had their good looks or personality going for them. Maybe I could have fit in if my dad hadn't been the crazy guy who was the laughingstock of the community.

Despite all the people who turned up their noses in our presence, there were still some folks who had hearts of true Christians. One of these families showed up one Christmas and did a beautiful thing, and through their kindness created one of my few good Christmas memories. Our cupboards were bare that year, a fact that my mom kept hidden from us. She did not know how there was going to be anything, even the smallest gift for us under the tree. As she wrestled with these worries, a family from our school community came to our house with bags of groceries and gifts. My gift was a pink sweater that I can still see as if it were yesterday. I wish I still had it. It became very special to me. Their visit felt surreal. Even now as I remember, I am blown away by this loving act. Their kindness and generosity meant the world to us, though they probably never realized the lasting impact it had on us.

My siblings and I did not fully understand the significance of that Christmas until we were older. It was not just the sweater; it was not just that our cupboards were no longer bare; it was that someone had been able to see past all that we were and recognize our need. They knew about my dad's antics, but they looked past that and saw us for who we were: a family.

These folks are still in our lives today and will always be in my heart. Through them I learned about paying it forward. That act of kindness was not just about the money they spent; it was the thoughtfulness and love behind the act that impacted us most. Beyond their tangible gifts was a gift far more valuable: the possibility that we were not as alone as we once thought.

CHAPTER SEVENTEEN

"Our greatest glory is not in never falling,
but in rising every time we fall."
—Confucius

My four years of high school seemed endless. Not much changed in my social life; I felt like I was peering through the window of school life from the outside. I never found school to be relaxing or stress-free; I felt like I had to be "on" all the time. While most of the kids in my class were fine, a few were mean. Sometimes it was subtle, but their attitude was always present, permeating everything and reminding me that I was different.

One of my least favorite places was the locker room at gym time. In the girls' locker room, I felt like Cinderella looking at her stepsisters.

I know all teenagers are critical of themselves, but to me, all my classmates seemed to be pretty, popular, and have cute clothes. I wanted cute days-of-the-week underwear like the ones some of the other girls wore. And while everyone else was chattering happily, I was off to the side with my only friend, dreading the next hour. Gym class was the bane of my existence, though I had no choice but to tolerate it. It made me feel inadequate, because I thought I didn't have an athletic bone in my body. While this may have been true, I still wish I had pushed myself to develop some skills without feeling so intimidated all the time.

This was the era in gym class when it was common for two students who were good athletes to pick the teams for whatever game was at hand. I was always the last one chosen, and the people on the team that got stuck with me would roll their eyes and sigh with disappointment. It was a little thing, but every time a team was chosen, a piece of my self-esteem disintegrated. When we played football, I would fervently pray that the ball wouldn't come near me. In baseball, I would pray that I could just hit the ball enough to not be struck out.

Then there were the physical fitness tests where you had to hang on a bar with your chin up—I think it was called the flexed arm hang. My chin and body did not seem to understand this; I was lucky if my chin made it over the bar as I slowly slid right off, frustrating me and further embarrassing me in front of everyone. Looking back on gym class, I was basically the female version of Greg Heffley, the main character in *Diary of a Wimpy Kid*.

Though I never felt like I fit in at school, I did have a quiet ambition: to be a class officer. It was obvious that my athletic skills wouldn't get me picked for sports teams, but I knew I could be a great class officer.

Class officers were chosen by the whole class. Students would suggest names of those who we thought would make a good president, vice president, secretary, historian, and so on. Then, with a list of names to choose from, we voted. Sitting in the last row of desks, second from the door, I would hold my breath every time a role was presented and names were suggested. I wanted someone to mention my name, but I would have had to stand with my hands in the air shouting, *"PICK ME,*

PLEASE PICK ME!!" to be noticed.

I felt invisible, as usual. Nobody ever suggested my name. I was disappointed, but I didn't see how it could have been any different.

One of my few good memories from school occurred during my last year. It was our senior class trip. We took a bus to a church camp in Michigan to go skiing for a few days. I had never even been to a ski slope, much less actually skied. But I watched others ski and figured, how hard could it be?

Those of us who had never skied were given a lesson. I'd been told that beginners would start on a "bunny hill," but what I saw did not fit the description of a bunny hill! I stood on top of what seemed to be a very steep hill, looking all the way down. Getting down that hill on skis was a nightmare ride I will never forget.

Somehow—falling, rolling, and screaming—I made it to the bottom without any broken limbs. A little boy, maybe four or five years old, skied confidently over to me on his little skis as I lay in the snow where I stopped. "Are you OK?" he asked.

I was beyond humiliated. Who thought that it was a good idea to use two narrow planks attached to awkward stiff boots for the purpose of risking one's life by going down a snowy, sometimes icy mountain? It wasn't until much later in life, after my children started skiing and snowboarding, that I tried again. Unsurprisingly, I was no better at it. In the chalet, by the fire with a good book was where I belonged.

Despite my failure on the slopes, the girls on the class trip actually talked to me as we hung out in the cabin in the evening. For a moment, I had the sense of belonging that I had always yearned for. That trip was one of the highlights of my high school experience.

Returning from our trip, the bus pulled into the school parking lot, which was filled with families ready to pick up their children. As I came around the corner of the bus, I saw Kumar bouncing out of our van, excited to see me. I was happy enough to see him, too, until I saw something behind him.

A family dog, barking and wagging its tail in delight at seeing a family member return—that was normal at a pickup like this. No one would have batted an eyelash. But we didn't have a dog.

We had GOATS! As my brother raced toward me, alongside of him ran a goat! My brother was beaming and excited to have Fancy Nancy with him to greet me.

I knew, of course, that we had goats. But why did they bring "my" goat (as defined by my dad) to pick me up from a school trip? Once again, I felt humiliated. Why could my family never just be normal?

Yes, we had goats. My dad wanted us to experience country life, despite the fact that we lived on the edge of town and not in the country. So, one day three goats arrived at our house, one for each of us. They were an addition to the ten chickens that were already living in our yard. I never knew if my dad consulted my mom on these random ideas of his or if he simply acted on impulse.

We didn't have a fenced yard, so how the chickens and goats did not wander away I do not know. Our dilapidated shed became a makeshift barn. My dad wanted us to experience gathering eggs from the hens and eating them fresh for breakfast. This did not happen. My brothers and I did not care to put our hands under the hens to grab the eggs, fearing we would get pecked. My dad never gathered the eggs either, so my poor mom had to add this to her list of things to do. Mom was not naturally an animal person and had never had experiences like this in her life, but her kind heart would not allow her to see these creatures neglected.

One of our aunt's came to visit and was excited to make fresh goat curry—I mean, *really* fresh. My siblings and I were appalled. We pleaded with my mom not to take the goats to the butcher, and eventually we found a farmer who was willing to take them in. The chickens, sadly, had a date with the butcher that they were not lucky enough to avoid. We begged our mom to not feed us those chickens. Somehow it seemed so wrong. Later we found out that my smart mom would mix some of our chickens from the yard with the store-bought chicken, and we were never the wiser.

TRANSITIONS

CHAPTER EIGHTEEN

"If your dreams don't scare you, they aren't big enough."
—Muhammad Ali

My four miserable years of high school finally came to an end. There were so many decisions to make, the biggest being: where would I go to university? *Whether* to go to university wasn't even a question; it was just assumed that I would go. As it turned out, I didn't even have to decide where to go. My parents had always intended to send me to Andrews University, our church's university in Michigan.

Though my mom said she was raising me to be an independent woman, many things in our family were still done with a traditional, old-school mentality. My mom would never have admitted it, but while I was going to university to get my degree, she was likely also hoping that I would find a nice Christian husband and get my "MRS" degree along with my B.A.

So many emotions filled me as I prepared to leave home for the first time. I had a lot of fears about the unknown. This was not like a sleepover—oh wait! I had never been on a sleepover. We were not even allowed to sleep over at our cousins' house.

One of the things that I was able to cross off my list of things to worry about was a roommate. One of the girls from my high school class asked me to be her roommate. I wasn't sure why. She was popular and cool; she had a boyfriend. But she did ask, so I accepted. I was more afraid of her disapproving of me as her roommate than I would have been if I had been paired with a perfect stranger.

There were so many little things I needed or wanted as I prepared to leave home for the first time. My future roomie showed me a picture of her comforter, dark blue on one side and a lighter blue on the other side. She wanted me to try to match it and told me where I could get one like it. My mom somehow found the money to get me everything I needed for university, plus a few extras, including that matching comforter.

I am sure my mom's heart was heavy as she helped me gather all the things that I needed to make a home away from her. I had fantasized about escaping this hell that was our family life for so long, yet as one foot was eager to step out, my other foot had a hard time doing so. I was stepping out without my mom and brothers. This world, with all its craziness and dysfunction, was the only world I knew.

What was I walking into? And what would happen to my mom and brothers? I had always carried them with me. We were a team. We stuck together. I left with my heart hurting as I hugged my brothers goodbye. My parents drove me the five hours to Michigan in our big brown Ford Econoline conversion van. That huge vehicle was filled with stuff that would make a dorm room my home for the next nine months.

My roommate and I decorated our small room. She was so much cooler than I was, and I found myself copying little things she did: buying Salon Selective shampoo and conditioner, Bonnie Bell lip gloss, and banana clips for my hair, among many other things. Our next-door neighbors were two other girls from our high school—again, girls I thought of as being super cool. I was so quiet and felt like such a loser. I was certain that my roommate must have felt like she had picked the short straw.

That first semester, homesickness hit hard. I missed home, my brothers, my mom, and even my dad. This new world was so big! I was not sure that I belonged here. I thought I was a misfit in high school, and this was a much bigger playing field.

My parents and Kumar came to Andrews to visit me on the second weekend of the school year, to surprise me for my nineteenth birthday. That same morning, my roommate had been showing me how to apply makeup—something I knew little about. So I was wearing eyeliner and mascara when I got a call asking me to come to the lobby. I am not sure who was more surprised: me seeing my parents there, or my mom seeing me with makeup on. She was so upset! With tears in her eyes, she told me that she had not sent me to college to learn to wear makeup and other "bad" things.

Eventually my mother calmed down, and I showed my family around. The university town had one traffic light, and, as you might imagine, there wasn't much to do. After driving around and showing them the campus, I asked if they would like to see where Muhammad Ali lived. His home was very close by and he would sometimes come to the university to socialize, sign autographs, and pass out his flyers on Islam.

Despite Ali being the Greatest of All Time, the folks in town respected him and his privacy. His was a gated property, and I assumed we would drive by, take a quick look from the gate, and continue on our way.

My dad's overzealousness should have been my first clue that this would not be the case. I didn't even realize he knew much about Ali. We made our way to Ali's street. His estate sat on a beautiful piece of property with iron gates at the entrance. What would most normal people do when they came to see his place? Exactly—they would look, comment among themselves, and then drive on. Normal people would not even consider driving onto the compound and up to the house, parking by the side door, and honking their horn over and over and over again.

Did you reread that? Yes, the gates were open, and my dear dad must have taken that as an invitation from Ali himself. Even as my dad was driving up the long driveway, Kumar and I begged him to leave. Have you ever had your parents do something so appalling that you wanted to crawl into a hole? As my dad started beeping the horn, I remember diving to the van floor. My brother followed suit.

How was this going to end? Where was the security? Why were the gates left open? My dad did not just beep the horn. It was beep! BEEP-BEEP! BEEP! The dogs outside the house were barking, obviously agitated. After another set of beeps, the door opened and a woman we later learned was Muhammad Ali's mother-in-law peered out the crack in the door in her bathrobe and asked if she could help us. My dad, without any shame or hesitation replied, "We have come all the way from India to see Muhammad Ali."

It was mortifying enough that we were intruding on this family's life. It was yet another thing to say that we came all the way from India just to do it. My dad did have a strong accent, so she may have believed we had literally just come from India. She was very kind, though. She told him that Ali was still asleep—it was early in the morning—but if we came back in a couple of hours, he might see us.

Exactly two hours later, we were back at the side door. Just as before, the dogs greeted us with barks that were meant to keep folks like my dad away. And yes, my dad began honking again.

This time the side door swung open and out came Muhammad Ali himself—the Greatest of All Time! He was so charming and gracious, and very welcoming, despite the fact that we were intruders. He quickly picked up on my dad's obnoxiousness and how uncomfortable my mom, Kumar, and I were. He engaged my brother and me in conversation, while at the same time taking little verbal jabs at my dad, which went over his head (probably because he had come all the way from India).

Ali did some magic tricks, gave us a tour of the compound, and even showed us where he worked out and prepared for fights. He then invited us into his home and gave us copies of the Quran, which he signed. He was gracious and posed for pictures with us.

They say a picture is worth a thousand words. I am not sure any picture can really express all my emotions as I posed with Muhammad Ali. I was embarrassed, nervous, in awe, and overwhelmed.

As I stepped away from my dysfunctional family life, I was going through a metamorphosis in baby steps. As the weeks went by, my comfort grew and I slowly began to find myself. I was not as big a loser as I thought. I was not ugly. I was not stupid. I was OK. There were people in this place who liked me and wanted to be with me. They laughed with me, offering friendship with no strings attached.

My fellow students came from many different ethnic backgrounds, and my family's economic status was not an issue, nor was it even apparent here in a boarding school. For the first time I found others much like me. We shared the same foods; we understood parental quirks and cultural things. We would often make simple Indian food and hang out until the wee hours. My friendships with my high school classmates grew too as we spent that time together, sharing our struggles and dreams, admitting to being homesick during those first months, and talking about our crushes or relationships.

I was a bit boy crazy, and there were so many boys who caught my attention. I did not date at this point; having a crush was exciting enough. But my attention was definitely more focused on my social life than on my education. There were many adjustments, but the pros of that first year in university outweighed the cons. I was finding myself and, more importantly, learning to love myself.

As my friendships grew, I learned that many families were dysfunctional. Not everyone had experienced the same combination of physical and emotional abuse that I had, but many of my friends' families were still damaging. I was not the only one to face challenges at home. I look back on this time and I am so grateful for the gift of friendship that God blessed me with—friendships that continue today and have stood the test of time.

CHAPTER NINETEEN

"It doesn't matter if your glass is half empty or half full.
Be thankful that you have a glass and grateful that
there is something in it."
—Unknown

I spent the summer after my freshman year back home in Dayton, working in the kitchen of a nearby retirement home. I began dating a guy I worked with, who had also gone to my high school and was a bit younger. It was exciting to experience all the "firsts" that most people had in high school. At nineteen years old, I had my first date, held a guy's hand, and had my first kiss. I loved all the things that came with dating. My brothers knew my boyfriend and my parents liked him. Life that summer was great. But as I returned to university, I ended this relationship amicably, knowing that we were heading down different paths, and yet I cherished all that had come from the relationship.

One of the reasons I enjoyed that summer was that there had been a major change in our family's living situation back home. It was around the time I left for university that, as I mentioned earlier, my parents started a business. They turned our family home into a group home for seniors, most of whom were Alzheimer's patients. My mom continued to work her shifts at the hospital, then came home and took care of the needs of the residents. Initially, my dad made some of the meals and did some caretaking as well. But eventually they were able to hire help. This gave my mom a much-needed break and left my dad free to do what he had always done best—disappear for the day.

With the family home turned into a care facility, my parents rented an apartment nearby, which provided a place for our family away from the group home. While I was away at college, my brothers had the apartment to themselves most of the time, going to the house for meals and to spend time with my mom. They enjoyed a freedom that I had never known, and once I was home for the summer, I was able to experience the more relaxed atmosphere of the apartment along with them.

One day at the end of that summer, my dad asked me to come out to the apartment's parking lot. He said he had a surprise for me. Surprises from my dad were unpredictable, often involving things like goats and chickens, so it was with much trepidation that I headed outside, with my siblings and my mom trailing behind me.

Out in the parking lot was a car. Dad showed it to me in a grandiose fashion, telling me that it was a gift. Now, this is going to sound very ungracious, but it was a four-door Ford sedan—a car that you might refer to as a boat. I didn't mind that it was older, but the color was a shade of green for which "atrocious" is too kind a word.

I was simultaneously touched and horrified. How was I going to drive that thing around? I would truly rather not have had a vehicle than to be seen in that … thing!

That was when I realized this was a joke of sorts for my dad. He handed me the key, not to the hideous green sedan, but to a blue Ford Escort wagon! I was so delighted—the Escort might as well have been a Porsche! It was an average used car, and while it might not have been the first choice for most college students, I was so grateful for my parents' generosity and kindness. It was so nice to have a vehicle to get around in, and it was a relief to no longer worry about finding a ride home from university. I felt blessed.

Chapter Twenty

*"We didn't realize we were making memories,
we were just having fun."*
—Winnie the Pooh

Returning to university was always something I looked forward to. The leaves started falling as the year began, and it meant another new beginning. I loved the lightness in my heart and the sense of being carefree. I was finding myself and redefining the "me" that had been invisible for so many years. God could not force change on my dad, but I was discovering that I could be happy outside of my dad's control.

I found myself blessed with deep and beautiful friendships that have withstood the test of time. After growing up without a sister and feeling lonely and isolated in high school, I loved life in the women's dorm. It was like having a dozen sisters to share joys and tears, laughter and secrets, hopes and dreams.

Reading through my journals from my college years, I am mortified to see how young and innocent—naïve—I really was. I had discovered a social freedom in university that most people experience in high school. It was all so innocent, but I was definitely "boy crazy," especially in my first and second years. The other girls I knew were all a bit boy crazy too, so I was probably more normal than I realized. I had a planner, the kind that most students used to keep track of projects and exam dates. I used mine to record which cute guys I saw and where I spotted them, if we made eye contact, and whether we spoke. I documented all my crushes.

Mealtime at the cafeteria was another time for socializing. It was a safe space that allowed for spying on the crush of the hour, checking out couples, catching up on the latest gossip, and just decompressing around our table of friends. In the dorms, we spent time hanging out together, eating Ramen, Taco Bell dollar menu items, and, when lucky, homemade food sent from our moms.

On Friday nights we got dressed up and headed to vespers. You might say we put on our "Sunday best" for the Friday evening worship program. Truth be told, we were not really dressing up for the program as much as to be seen. I loved sharing clothes with other girls in the dorm—the sisters I had never had.

Late night conversations deepened our friendships, as we shared pain, heartaches, and joys. This sharing opened my eyes to the realization that everyone has a story. Suddenly my load felt lighter just knowing that while my heartaches were big, my friends knew hardships and heartaches too.

During my freshman year at Andrews I had bumped into a good-looking Indian guy in a doorway. He was heading out of the copy room while I was going in. He had curly black hair, a low beard, and a mustache. I said "hi" and was taken aback by what I perceived as his rudeness—he walked past me without giving me the time of day. A few of my fellow students had already made my list of rude, arrogant, obnoxious people, and I lumped this Indian guy in with them: he was kind of cute, but he was rude and stuck up.

My friends occasionally pointed him out to me during assembly or chapel, but I had already decided I didn't like him. It was a new thing for me to see so many people of different ethnic backgrounds, especially of Indian descent. I was attracted to several Indian guys on campus. Each semester, various crushes occupied my thoughts. I was so sheltered and I'd had only a handful of male acquaintances in high school. University life was like being released from a lion's den into a world of all sorts of species.

In my sophomore year, it was easy to jump back into the space that I loved. I still had my roommate, Shelley, from high school, and our chemistry was easy. My shyness had lessened and I continued to slowly discover who I really was. One of my male cousins, Kishore, also enrolled at Andrews that year and was there with me. Since most of my cousins lived in Maryland and we didn't get to spend much time together, this felt like a special gift.

Andrews University was multicultural. It also included many graduate programs, which meant there were many older families and groups who embraced the younger students. Shann, another Indian friend I was blessed with, had more of an "in" with this older group. I remember the first time he took me to an Indian Society potluck: the spread before me was plentiful, with so many mouth-watering rice and curry dishes, a taste of home. This broadened my scope and understanding of my culture and the people with whom I had so much in common.

Growing up, aside from my cousins, we had limited contact with other Indian families. Being with other people who appreciated the same traditions and customs was comforting and refreshing. No explanation was needed.

On one occasion, the folks from this Indian Society approached a few of us to help with a program that would require us to wear the national dress. All the guys wore turbans and the girls wore saris. The group included Shann, my cousin Kishore, another Indian girl we were friends with, and an Indian guy that Shann and Kishore knew who sometimes came to the Indian potlucks. He seemed familiar, and I soon realized that he was the same "stuck up" guy I had bumped into in the copy room during my freshman year. His name was Sanj.

He had the same black curly hair, low cut beard, and mustache that I remembered from our first encounter, but there was something different about him. Then it hit me! He was smiling and friendly. That aloofness seemed to have disappeared. And he was still cute.

The Indian Society program was my first real interaction with Sanj. As the five of us hung out waiting for our part in the program, my friendship with him began.

I found myself crushing on Sanj in a big way. He had just come out of a relationship that had broken his heart and he had no interest in me romantically, as he was still licking his wounds. To Sanj I was an immature young friend, but one with a lot of energy. He enjoyed our friendship and the distraction that hanging out with our mutual friends brought. I had to accept this reality, yet my heart always seemed to hold a special spot for this curly-haired friend of mine.

I was registered to take Philosophy 101 and was not really overjoyed at the thought, until I walked into the first class and saw Sanj there too. Funny how it turned out to be my favorite class that semester! I am not sure what was said in the lectures, but I often found myself doodling little hearts around the words "Reema and Sanj"!

I loved hanging out with this group of friends: Kishore, Shann, the other girl, and of course Sanj. The five of us continued to spend time together when we were not studying. Sanj was an RA (residence assistant) in the men's dorm. He was responsible, studious, and focused. It was his last year, and he would graduate with a degree in communication disorders on his way to becoming an audiologist. While I did have a crush on him, I also really enjoyed our friendship and was able to keep the crush under control.

It was not uncommon for me to call Sanj, Kish, and Shann and beg them to go out on a Saturday night and do something. The answer was often that they were studying. I was always appalled by that answer. Saturday night was the one night when we could legitimately escape the books. But sometimes the answer was yes. While we did many things locally and cheaply, there were also occasional outings that took us away from the little town of Berrien Springs.

Sanj—the curly-haired, bearded guy, whose laughter I just loved—was definitely a creature of habit. He often wore a uniform of sorts: a black and white broad striped shirt with a bright yellow zip-up sweatshirt and black pants. I have so many memories of him wearing that outfit. Being a university student, money was scarce. Girls had no trouble sharing clothing so our wardrobes expanded easily. I guess guys didn't do that kind of thing.

I was pretty high energy; Sanj might modify that description to "super crazy energy." Looking back, I realize I was just giddy with the freedom of being *me*. For so many years I had been restricted, unconsciously paralyzed by the fear that the real me would be ostracized, either because of my dad or just the lack of acceptance from my peers. The release of the real me was something that slowly blossomed as I continued to feel safe. This little group of mine was safe. I knew I was loved and protected—at least by Shann and my cousin. Sanj still seemed to have some of his barriers up, yet I was sure that if the boogie man came after me, he would have stepped up.

Shann was my guardian angel who rescued me time after time. He was studying auto mechanics, and my car was not very dependable. One time when I went to Chicago to visit a girlfriend, my car betrayed me, leaving me stranded. I had no one to call. My parents would have scolded me for taking this trip, and anyway they could do nothing from a few states away. I gave Shann my location and he drove two hours to come and rescue me. Little did I know, I had given him the wrong directions—I was stranded east of the highway but had told him to go west!

In those days before cell phones, Shann had no choice but to go back when he couldn't find me. I was able to contact him again, and even though it was close to midnight and despite my mistake, this amazing friend headed back out to rescue me. He tinkered with my car, got it running again, and followed me back to campus.

The five of us created many memories. We traveled to Sanj's home in Simcoe, Ontario, a couple of hours from Toronto. I have no idea why my parents let me go on a six-and-a-half-hour trip to Canada; maybe it was because my cousin was with me.

That trip was full of fun and lasting memories. Sanj's parents were hospitable, offering lots of food and making us all feel welcome as we stayed the night. Sanj's younger brother, Raj, joined in on the fun as well. I do not know how we all fit into Sanj's old car, which we jokingly called the "Ferrari"—likely without seatbelts and on top of each other! Though our time together lasted only a couple of semesters, I adored these guys and considered them my family. I was heartbroken as that year came to an end and I had to say goodbye. All three of the guys would be going to Maryland; Kishore and Shann lived there, and Sanj was going to George Washington University for graduate school.

CHAPTER TWENTY-ONE

"That which does not kill us makes us stronger."
—Friedrich Nietzsche

Meanwhile at home, my brothers continued to grow up, both emotionally and physically. The abuse my dad directed at them was now more verbal and emotional than physical, as he could no longer predict my brothers' reactions. My brothers reached out for help, sharing stories of abuse at home with the school chaplain whom they trusted. Their courage amazed me. Both my brothers developed a close relationship with "Pastor" and seemed to find some solace in having someone to confide in.

Rajiv finished high school and headed to Washington state to attend a Christian university. Just as I was doing at Andrews, he was able to start finding himself at university without the restrictions of our home life. Kumar was still in high school, but life was definitely a different journey for him. He fit in; he was outgoing and social. He had friends and showed leadership skills at a young age.

Kumar continued to develop a close relationship with Pastor and shadowed him, as he was the student chaplain. Pastor was a staff member who was loved by the students and had a very open relationship with them. It was common for students to congregate in his office and at his home on the weekends. This man was very affectionate and loving and seemed to know how to fill the needs of the students. He was married, and he and his wife had one son. His wife was a nurse and must have worked the 3:00–11:00 p.m. shift, which left Pastor with their son, whom he would bring to school activities. Students loved the little boy and Pastor never really lacked for babysitters. Their little boy was loved and doted on.

Sometimes when I was home on weekends, I would tag along with my brother and his crew. One of the times when I tagged along, we were traveling somewhere in a van as the team led out in an evening service. Pastor seemed overly friendly, like he was trying too hard with me. I left thinking that something about the encounter felt a bit "off," but I was still grateful for this man being a positive figure in my brother's life.

My brothers and I appreciated the apartment our parents rented, as it gave us a place of our own away from the elder care home. One spring break, when I was home from college and my brothers and I were all at the apartment, the phone rang and Kumar answered it. His tone and the look on his face made us aware that it was something serious. After prompting from us, he told us the caller was a lady who worked for my parents at the group home. She had quit, and she wanted us to know why.

The help my parents hired were often people from the downtown core; they were eager to make money and were good workers. My dad usually drove this woman to the bus stop after work, and she would make her way home on the city bus. Over the phone, this woman told my brother that my dad had offered her rides home and had been inappropriate with her. He had apparently taken her to our apartment when no one else was there. She described the apartment in accurate detail, so we knew she wasn't lying. He made sexual advances toward her. It had happened more than once. She let us know she could not work under these conditions.

The three of us sat in the living room of the little apartment, shell-shocked and stunned after Kumar told us what the woman had said on the phone. I was sitting on the same sofa where I had had my first kiss, struggling to process what I'd just heard. We all wondered if our dad was capable of this kind of disgusting behavior, but sadly, the answer was apparent to us.

We were always protective of my mom, partly because of her naivety and vulnerability. My brothers did not hold my mom as accountable as I did. Maybe because I was older, maybe because I had experienced much more, I had started to resent my mom. I felt like I had been forced into the role of being her partner and sidekick, rather than simply being her daughter. She had never made changes to protect us or herself. Nothing ever changed.

My brothers didn't seem as surprised by my dad's actions as I was. We discussed whether we should tell our mother, and we all agreed that she needed to know. But who would tell her? I was the obvious choice so, once again, the responsibility of taking care of her fell on me.

Lucky me! How could I tell my mom that her abusive husband was now going outside our home to sexually harass one of his employees—and who knows who else?

I was sick to my stomach. I did not know how to tell my mom. My dad had hurt her so much, time and again. Would this be the last straw?

That thought gave me strength. The shed where our three goats had lived a couple years earlier had been converted into a laundry room/storage space. Winter was on its way out and spring was in the air. I went into the laundry room and told my mom I needed to tell her something.

"What is it?" She was putting a load of clothes in the washer.

This was so hard. I felt like I needed to vomit and my eyes filled with tears. It took an enormous amount of courage for me to repeat the accusations.

My mom didn't appear shocked or surprised. In fact, she hardly reacted at all. I could have been telling her about the weather. "This woman has told me these things before," my mother assured me. "But she is known for lying. She's making this up. Don't worry—everything will be OK."

The whole disturbing incident was nicely swept under the rug. We never brought it up again.

CHAPTER TWENTY-TWO

"A true friend is someone who thinks that you are a good egg even though he knows that you are slightly cracked."
—Bernard Meltzer

During my third year at Andrews, my roommate was again someone from high school. Linda had reached out to me on my first day of high school when, as she recalls, I looked like I wanted to be swallowed up by my locker. I don't remember how we came to be roommates, but the time we spent living together led to a lifelong friendship. We talked openly about boys, our families, and all things in between. On Friday nights we would often nap until late in the evening, then chat until the wee hours. I shared my pain about our family, especially my longing for a relationship with my dad.

These conversations led me to reach out to my dad. How could I expect change if he was unaware of my desires? I handwrote a heartfelt, eight-page letter to my dad, making myself totally vulnerable. I told him that I wanted to have a good relationship with him, and that I wanted to be sad to be leaving his home someday when I got married. I wanted him to know how much I loved him and needed his love and affirmation.

I was terrified of his response. Would he be mad, or would he be touched? Would he finally tell me he loved me? Weeks went by with no response of any kind. I didn't even know if he had received the letter.

As more time passed and I still heard nothing from my dad, I regretted sending the letter. Obviously, his silence was his answer. Finally, during a phone call with my mom, I asked her if my dad had received my letter.

"He did," she confirmed. "He even gave it to me to read."

So, he had gotten my letter—but he never ever said anything about it. That hurt. The wall that was slowly being built between us grew a little higher.

One long weekend, my friends and I loaded up my Ford Escort wagon and headed back to Dayton. We were excited for a break and enjoying the ride with chatter that can only happen between friends. When we were about an hour from home, I heard an unpleasant sound from the engine and pulled over to the side of the highway. The car seemed to be having a temper tantrum. My dear, faithful wagon refused to budge. We locked up the vehicle, walked to the closest exit, and fed the payphone the required quarters to call home. The plan was to wait for my dad to come rescue us. That was just what a dad did, wasn't it?

My dad came to the phone, listened to my saga and said coldly, "This is your problem. You should have known better than to drive the car home if it is not dependable. You will have to find a way to get yourself and the car home."

My dad had done a lot of things that left my mouth open, but this was absurd. He had to be joking. There were four of us young ladies stranded on the side of the highway, an hour from home.

He hung up on me.

How humiliating it was to tell my friends that my dad refused to come to my rescue and to admit that he had just hung up on me! My dad's love and decency had a switch that he was able to turn off and on. How could anyone leave a bunch of nineteen-year-old girls stranded in the middle of nowhere? My mom was at work, unaware of my dad's antics, and I had no way of reaching her. My girlfriend Linda called her dad, who did what dads do and came to pick us up, driving all of us to our various homes.

Linda's dad behaved like a real father. I was so jealous. Not only did he step up to the plate by rescuing us but he also drove back with his son in their vehicle and towed my car to my house.

As for my dad, he had no shame. He came out as my roommate's dad and brother towed the car into our yard and chatted with them as if this was the most natural thing. How he was able to look them in the eye was beyond my comprehension. I was mortified. I was beyond hurt. I felt another few bricks go up around my heart.

The one year I roomed with Linda seemed much longer (in a good way!) because we grew so close during that time. Our lives were completely opposite. To me, Linda seemed to have a charmed life. Her family was of West Indian descent; her dad was a Ph.D. nuclear physicist; they lived in the "right" neighborhood; they were well respected and fit into the bubble that was our community. She never seemed to worry about money and was secure in who she was. People were drawn to Linda and loved her. I was her shadow, but I wasn't jealous of her. I loved her too much to begrudge her anything, yet I was still wistful as I viewed her seemingly easy life.

Linda had gone to the same high school I did for two years, then transferred to a Christian boarding school on the outskirts of Toronto—the same school that Sanj and many of our peers attended. In university she studied occupational therapy, while I majored in education. We didn't have any classes together until one semester we were delighted to discover that basket weaving—yes, basket weaving—was a required class for both of us.

Our behavior in that class made me realize that it was probably a blessing that we only had one class together. Basket weaving was on Wednesdays from 6:00–9:00 p.m. that winter semester. Michigan winters were no joke, but cuteness trumped practicality, so I don't recall ever wearing a winter coat. Boots were also out of the question—we wore Keds without laces even in that frigid weather, walking across campus to our basket weaving class, and amusing ourselves with innocent silliness.

The ties that bound us in college have only grown over the years. After our year as roommates, Linda headed to Howard University to finish her undergraduate studies. Another of my beloved friends was heading to Maryland.

CHAPTER TWENTY-THREE

*"Sometimes the only way around suffering
is to go straight through it."*
—Anik Sarkar

During my last summer before finishing university, Rajiv and I were both at home, while Kumar was away working at summer camp. One day, my dad lost it with my mom. I am not sure what sparked his rage on this occasion, but by this time I knew it didn't have to be anything specific. He screamed at my mom, waving a broomstick and telling her, "I'm going to shove this down your throat! I'm going to kill you!!"

I realized we needed the police to intervene. My dad was over the edge and anything could occur. The last two times we had called the police, my dad had calmed down by the time they arrived and was always able to manipulate the situation. Despite the fact that the police had not been helpful before, I knew we needed outside intervention at this moment.

As the police arrived, I looked at my mom. Despite my concern for her, I couldn't keep the irritation, disgust, and anger from my voice as I asked her, "Why are you staying with him?"

For so long she had used the excuse that she stayed "because of us." But we were all young adults now, and soon we would all be out of the house.

She looked at me, desperation in her eyes. "If I go, will you come with me?"

Rajiv and I didn't hesitate. We helped my mom grab some of the things she needed, while the police held my dad at bay. He continued to rant to them as we climbed into our big brown Ford Econoline. My brother and I quit our summer jobs that day, and the three of us headed to my mom's sister's house in Maryland.

I was so proud of my mom. She had done it! She had finally left my dad! Today we were safe. Tomorrow we would tackle what came next. I felt so free and so proud of my mom for finally freeing herself from the shackles my dad had placed on her.

That freedom lasted two days. It took two days for my dad to get to her. He called her and told her that if she did not come back, he was going to drink cyanide and kill himself.

I rolled my eyes as my mom told me this. "Tell him to go ahead." I knew he was a chicken. "He'll never really do it, and if he does, it's no loss to you." I begged her not to go back. She had the resources and support to start a life in Maryland.

Then he called again, changing tactics. This time he told her that he was going to report her for abandoning the seniors at their house.

"If you go back, you are choosing *him* over *us*—your children," I told her.

The feeling of utter betrayal as my mom went back to her abuser was one I never have forgotten. In that moment, I lost respect for my mom.

CHAPTER TWENTY-FOUR

"Sometimes God sends us angels disguised as friends."
—Unknown

While Linda was in high school in Ontario, the school's assistant dean of men, David Knight, and his family, befriended her. Like Linda's family, the Knights were from Barbados. To our good fortune, they moved to Andrews University, where David became the associate dean of men. They had a cute little red brick house right on campus and their doors were always open. David and his lovely wife, Juliet, who was a nurse, also had two little ones, Jono (Jonathan) and Jess (Jessica). Linda introduced me to them and they immediately embraced me.

The Knights welcomed students into their home, and their fridge was stocked with delicious leftovers that had us salivating before we even got through the front door. Since they were of West Indian descent, they had rice and curry that always spoke to my belly. Juliet made the best lasagna, macaroni salad, green bean casserole, and many other dishes. Jono and Jess filled their home with silliness that only a two- and four-year-old could. Saturday nights often found Linda and me sprawled out on the Knights' basement carpet watching movies together. There was such innocence and a beautiful love that flowed from them.

David and Juliet invited me to live with them the following year. I would help out with their two children, and in return I could live with them with free room and board. This was a gift from God, and I firmly believe I received the better end of this deal. Along with providing my room and board, God was teaching me about family, and about loving, healthy relationships.

My room was in the basement—a spacious room right beside the family room. Shortly after I moved in, I was unpacking when I heard a distinct sound that was all too familiar to me. My heart began pounding as I heard kids shrieking, and a body falling to the floor over and over again. What was I to do? What had I gotten myself into?

I couldn't just stay in my room. I prayed up a storm, asking God for strength and protection as I tiptoed up the stairs into the kitchen to peek into the living room. As I drew nearer, I again heard the sound of a body being tossed around with loud shrieks. I took a deep breath looked around the corner and let out a huge sigh of relief. The children were climbing up on the sofa and jumping off repeatedly! What I had heard was the thuds as they jumped, and their cries of delight. I realized then how much the abuse at home had traumatized me.

Life with the Knights was a breath of fresh air. I loved the kids, Jono and Jess. Juliet was so motherly and protective. David was nurturing and encouraging, enabling me to spread my wings. They became like a second family, a relationship that has endured and grown over the years and continues to this day. Jono and Jess are grown now; David and Juliet are ageless. Our families are intertwined, and my own children have developed a relationship with them. This family was a gift to me from God; they became my family.

CHAPTER TWENTY-FIVE

"A playful path is the shortest road to happiness."
—Bernie DeKoven

I kept in touch with "the guys," as I affectionately called them, after they left Andrews. I saw Shann, Kish, Sanj, and Linda on my visits to see family in Maryland. Sanj also had family near Andrews, so he would return to the area occasionally.

For my twenty-first birthday, the guys came back and surprised me! I was so thrilled and very touched. That Saturday night they took me out in the "Ferrari" to induct me into adulthood. I was delighted. I loved these guys so much that I was happy to agree to their rules for my birthday celebration—I had to do whatever they said.

Our first stop was the video store in town. This tiny university town had only one traffic light and no fast food restaurants. Wherever you went, everyone saw you. The guys told me to go into the video store and rent an embarrassing adult movie. I was so innocent that I had never watched an R-rated movie, and the guys knew it. They took great pride in "breaking my innocence." I rented my first and last pornographic movie. We never intended to watch it—and we didn't—but it had the intended effect of embarrassing me.

Next was the liquor store. I was told to go in and purchase a specific liquor. I didn't drink and had never consumed a beverage stronger than a Diet Coke. Fortunately, I only had to purchase it, not drink it. The last stop in our little town was to the drug store, where the guys sent me in to buy condoms. They laughed at my mortification as they blew up some of them to use as birthday balloons, which they flew out the car window.

After those three tasks, we left our little town and headed to South Bend, where the mall and restaurants were. We went to the mall, where the last challenge was to pick up a guy that they picked out for me. I did it, but not in the way they intended. Instead of attempting to pick the guy up, I walked up to him, chatted, and clued him in on the foolishness we were up to. He was very sweet and played along.

I accomplished all the steps to fulfill my friends' random criteria for this rite of passage. Later, we hung out at Sanj's aunt's house. The weekend was fun and meant a lot to me, just to know that they had all made the effort to be there to celebrate my birthday.

The previous summer, I had been in a friend's wedding in Wisconsin. I had forgotten my camera and one of the groomsmen, who was my partner at the wedding, had taken it home with him, knowing he could give it back to me when school began. Over the summer we wrote letters back and forth that were full of light banter. We grew to like each other as we corresponded. The interest was mutual, and as we both returned to school a couple of weeks early, we were able to hang out and spend some time together.

The guys came for my birthday about a week after my groomsman friend and I had hung out. I was excited for the guys to meet him, and for him to meet my guys. Strangely, Sanj didn't seem to like my new friend, despite the fact that he had not yet met him, and unkindly nicknamed him Horse-face, because of his long face.

I had told my new friend all about my group of friends and was excited to introduce him to my buddies. Yet before they had a chance to meet, he told me that "this thing between us" was not going to work out. He said he wasn't comfortable dating someone of a different race.

I loved taking pictures and always had my camera with me. After the guys left campus following my birthday weekend, I took the film to the campus bookstore to have my pictures developed. I paid for them and was flipping through the pictures while waiting for my change. The first couple of photos were not mine. They were very inappropriate pictures that included parts of the male anatomy that are not usually exposed. Horrified, I started to let the cashier know that they were not mine, but as I flipped through the pictures, I realized that the rest were mine.

I was confused and concerned as to where these few pictures came from. I went home to show David Knight the pictures and express my concern. It seemed that these X-rated "selfies" had been taken by a white male, and I was disgusted that he did so with my camera! The only possibility I could think of was that the pictures had been taken by my seemingly innocent groomsman friend—a white male—who had had my camera over the summer. That thought was very disturbing!

I discovered the truth when one of the guys started questioning me about my prints. They were laughing so hard that it was obvious who the culprits were! Raj, Sanj's brother, had been with us at his aunt's house after my birthday celebration. In clandestine fashion, he had snuck off and taken pictures of pictures out of an artistic photography book that his cousin had. Raj knew how innocent and naive I was; he had taken these pictures to mess with me and then promptly forgotten about them. Mission accomplished!

CHAPTER TWENTY-SIX

"Ninety percent of the time, rape is done by someone you know.
Not a creepy man in the alley."
—Andrea Cooper

My last year of university was another year of fun and making wonderful memories. For the last year and a bit, I had been dating a young man named Ed, and thought that I might be in love with him. As we said goodbye at the end of that school year, I was sad and unsure of the future.

When I first started university, I majored in business at my dad's insistence. It was not for me. I hated numbers and barely passed accounting. So instead, I followed my heart and switched to a degree in education. As a little girl, I had played teacher. I had always loved children, and I couldn't wait to have a houseful of my own. Changing my major set me back a semester, and I still had my student teaching to complete before graduation.

I decided to do my student teaching at home in Dayton. Kumar was finishing his last year in high school, and I would be able to save money by living at home. It was convenient and familiar; I could complete this practicum at the elementary school connected to my old high school.

For three months I student taught under the supervision of an amazing teacher who taught in a grade three and four combined class. I loved this age and stage. I also enjoyed hanging out with my youngest brother and one of my dearest friends, Ellen, who still lived in town. She was busy as a young mom and wife, and our lives were very different, yet we still found time to hang out occasionally.

After my student teaching was completed, I had nothing to do until August when I would graduate. I was contacted by a denominationally affiliated school in Indiana; they were looking for someone to fill in for a teacher who had taken a leave of absence. It was a one-room schoolhouse with grades one through eight taught by one teacher. They offered a trailer home in the middle of a cornfield that would serve as my new residence.

I took the job, but my life in the trailer lasted maybe a week. I was too social to live in the middle of nowhere, and I was petrified to be alone. My parents lived an hour away, so I made the choice to move back home and commute.

While I was working at this temporary teaching job, my college boyfriend and I broke up. Distance was certainly a factor, but we also had vastly different ideas of what we wanted from life. Still, I was devastated. I had gone from being surrounded by friends at university, to living with my parents in a town where I had only one friend. Kumar didn't have a driver's license and I didn't have a life. He generously allowed me to tag along with his friends, most of whom I had known since they were little children.

Without much of a social life, I got involved helping "Pastor," the school chaplain, plan events for the students. Over time, Pastor and I developed a friendship. He knew about our complicated family life; he knew my dad and knew about the abuse we grew up with, since my brothers had turned to him for support while they were in school. He was engaging and empathetic.

Not only was he everything I believed a pastor should be—kind, gentle, and a charismatic speaker who loved God—Pastor also seemed to be exactly what a father and husband should be. He listened to me when I shared my pain and heartache about breaking up with my boyfriend. He understood and said the right things; he told me it was my ex's loss. He built me up and in my brokenness I believed his words.

One Sabbath, leaving church, I ran into Pastor with his wife and son. As we talked, he leaned over and whispered in my ear that I looked really nice. I was momentarily taken aback, yet it didn't seem out of the ordinary for him.

Pastor's office was a common spot for students to lounge. He was very complimentary and physical with the students. It was not uncommon to see female students resting on him, sitting on him, being very touchy and feely. When evening programs were finished, students often headed over to Pastor's home to hang out. We thought of his home as a safe and comfortable place. His wife would come home from work and head upstairs, seemingly accustomed to the constant company. His son was showered with love and attention from everyone.

What happened next confused and troubled me. As I think back on those events, I find myself turning to the pages of the journal I kept back then, to see how I reacted in the moment, without the filter of the years that have passed since then.

Journal, 2/25/1992:

This was a weekend that was very confusing to me. This was a weekend that Kumar was away. I had just dropped him off at the school and stopped in to say hi to whomever was left. "Pastor," or BR (as I will refer to him here) stopped me and asked if I was coming to that evening program and I replied probably. He told me that he hoped I did. Having nothing else to do, I went. It was all normal, BR asked me to watch his son during the event and when it was over we all left. What was weird was BR calling me later that night, knowing Kumar wasn't home. This was weird but he said, "We still never got a chance to talk." The conversation really had no direction at first and then he started to talk about my dad. He obviously knew stuff because he was supporting my brothers over a period of time. He then said, "I think you're very special and someday when I gather enough courage, I'll share how I feel about you." WHAT?

BR told me he wanted to see me again that weekend, before or after the basketball game. After an obvious pause, I replied OK, not sure what else to say. He caught me off guard. He obviously knew I was just responding reflexively and so he said, "Is it? Is it really OK?"

In my journal, I mentioned that I was not sure what Pastor meant when he said he wanted to share how he felt about me. I ended up pushing those questions aside, trying not to think about it.

I confided in Ellen about my confusion about Pastor. What did all this "stuff" mean? She told me that two weeks earlier she had heard he was involved in an extramarital affair. I was devastated to hear this about a man I idolized as a pastor, husband, and father. I didn't know whether to believe it. Looking back, I suppose I chose not to believe it.

That Monday, Pastor called Kumar to talk with him. On Tuesday, he called and I answered. "I cleared my schedule for you on Saturday night and you didn't show up," he told me.

Again, I was caught off guard. "OK," was all I said. I hadn't really felt any need to meet with him on Saturday night, and I felt like he had put me in an awkward position.

I saw him again that Thursday, as I picked up Kumar from school. He held my hand and looked at me in a way that made me uncomfortable.

This is what I wrote in my journal:

I am so confused about Pastor. I know he is safe because he is married and they have their kid. He is a pastor and listening to him, he obviously loves God. Despite the confusion, I do feel safe around him. He's so "free" with everyone.

Journal, 3/4/1992

Pastor left a note to meet him at Taco Bell. Nothing special, just ate and chatted and played with his son. Pastor asked if I wanted to go to Vic Tanny gym. I said no. My thoughts are all over the place. Missing my ex.

Over the next few weeks, Pastor continued to call and invite me to hang out. With the exception of the visit to Taco Bell, I never accepted his invitations to hang out unless we were with my brother or in a group. His wife asked me to babysit a few times and I did so gladly. I enjoyed their child and had nothing better to do, and I appreciated the pocket money.

The last time I babysat for them was April 16, 1992. I watched their son as I usually did. This time BR arrived home before his wife. He started chatting as I got ready to leave. He said he had to put his son into the bath. "But I'm getting my things together to go on a trip," he added. "Keep me company while I pack."

The next thing I knew, Pastor was on top of me. Fear gripped me. I was just a little thing, no more than 105 pounds. I was unable to stop him. He had me pinned, with my arms under him. He forced himself in me. He didn't bother to undress me, instead he forced himself through the leg of my orange knee-length shorts.

I begged him to stop. "You're hurting me!" I cried. "Please, please stop! I'm a virgin!!"

"I won't go in all the way," he replied coldly. As if that made it all OK.

That is all I remember. I am not sure how I made it home. I have no memory of leaving his place, getting home, or going into the apartment. My memory of that night skips forward to the bathroom at home. I sat on the toilet. My legs hurt. I looked down at my panties. There was the red stain. I had lost my virginity. I had just been raped.

I am not sure how long I sat there. Kumar eventually came banging on the door. "Hurry up! I need to get in the bathroom!"

My brother's words snapped me out of my daze and I left the bathroom. I had been raped. What was I going to do next?

I thought of calling the police, but as quickly as that thought came, it vanished. The police had never helped us in the past. They didn't care that my mom had been beaten black and blue. They hadn't cared when my dad threatened to kill us. Why would they care that I had been raped by a pastor? The police were not an option.

I had always told my close girlfriends everything; there were no boundaries between us. Now, for the first time, I felt truly alone. I whimpered to God, but I felt like I had no right to turn to Him. *It's my fault*, I reproached myself. My gut had been telling me to run. How had I been so stupid? How had I let this happen?

I was completely alone. I felt too guilty and ashamed to turn to God. My parents were not emotionally present. I wasn't sure I could even tell my girlfriends this. How could they possibly understand this when I didn't understand it myself?

I spent a lot of time in bed over the days that followed, curled up in a ball, crying, yearning for death. I pleaded with God to just take me. What if I was pregnant? *HOW IS THIS POSSIBLE?!* I silently screamed over and over.

I didn't know what I would do when I saw BR again—but when I did, he acted as if nothing had happened. I wanted to scream, to slap him, or to avoid him at all costs, but I did none of those things. Alone and traumatized, I was in a deep fog, and I did and said nothing. Any response I could have made seemed pointless and meaningless. He had done it; he had snared me in his trap. I had lost it all. Who cared?

I later learned that I was not the only young woman in our community with whom BR had acted inappropriately. That spring, not long after I was raped, the school hosted a youth rally. The visiting students slept in designated classrooms, and the local students stayed there overnight to oversee the visit and accommodate the needs of the guests. LB, a young girl who was a friend of our family, was sleeping in BR's office when BR came in, despite seeing her sleeping there. Alone with her in the room, he asked her, "Do you know how people keep warm in the cold? They take off their clothes and lie together."

After the youth rally, LB told my brother Kumar about this comment. Kumar, who at this time had no idea what had happened to me, was angry enough to go to BR's house and give him a letter, calling him out on his behavior. Kumar warned BR that if he didn't get his act together, Kumar would take things to the next level.

Another incident I learned about occurred when BR called one of the students into his office with the pretense of an assignment. Before she knew what was happening, BR kissed her. Shocked, she slapped him and walked out the door. She was someone who, like me, came from the "wrong side of the tracks." She was living with her aunt. When this incident was reported to the principal, he asked the girl, her aunt, and BR into his office. With BR sitting right across from her, she was to tell her story. It was BR's word against hers. Her aunt chose to let things go and moved her to a different school. Clearly, what happened to me was part of a pattern of behavior for BR, though his assault on me was by far the most serious.

In many ways, the aftermath was harder for me to understand than the rape itself. I felt like I was no longer living in my own body. The fog was impenetrable. I was broken and had let go, willing to freefall until it all ended in death or whatever other horror might come my way. This monster had broken me and now had me flopping around like a puppet on a string.

I still struggle with my actions after the rape. I remember that he acted as if nothing had happened, yet he continued to hurt me. He told me that he loved me and wished we could be together. "Would you go away with me for the weekend?" he asked. It was as if he was trying to make me his. Was he trying to make this vile act acceptable by turning it into some kind of a romance? I didn't know how to deal with any of this, but I also didn't agree to go away with him.

Another time, he grabbed me and (while holding his son) tried to force my face onto him to pleasure him. It went far enough to reinforce my sense of powerlessness and my inability to regain control. Why didn't I run? It was as if I wanted something bad to happen to me, like I deserved more bad things to happen to me.

He knew he had broken me.

It was only years later, after going through counseling, that I gained a better understanding of the hold he had over me. I came to understand that my experience was not unique; in fact, it was quite common in cases like this. It would take years of counseling for me to really understand the psychology of the perpetrator. Once again, as with the abuse in my childhood, I asked God to change the situation, but instead he gave me the strength to move forward.

It has taken more than three decades for the grown me to begin making sense of this experience and release the guilt and anger I felt toward my younger self. Sharing this nightmare with my closest friends over that period of time actually ended up making me feel worse rather than better. My friends couldn't relate; they had never been in a situation remotely close to this. While they responded with love, their words hurt more than they helped at that point.

As I continued on my journey of healing, I had to really open my heart and feel for my younger self. As a young woman I was alone, yearning for the love of a father like those I saw around me. I was always drawn to teachers and pastors who seemed to be substitute father figures, men whom I deemed safe and trustworthy.

When I look back at BR's victims, they were all girls who, like me, lacked a "normal" father figure. His targets were vulnerable and had a story he knew well, as they had trusted and confided in him. They all had a look that he must have found appealing. I have learned that perpetrators such as BR groom their victims. It was a skill set that he had mastered. After years of counseling, I have finally come to understand that the younger me had been groomed by BR. There was nothing I could have done in that moment, as he pinned me down and came in for the kill.

HOPE

Chapter Twenty-Seven

"Let us not love with words or speech
but with actions and in truth."
—1 John 3:18, NIV

Not knowing how to escape the hell I found myself living, I seized the chance to move to Maryland that summer and take a course. I had extended family there I could stay with, as well as a few close girlfriends. There was so much going on with all my family and friends that I lost myself in it instead of dwelling on what had happened to me.

A little more than four months had passed since I was raped. I survived the summer, just putting one foot in front of the other. In August I traveled back to Andrews University for my graduation. I was also still wounded by my ex-boyfriend Ed, and I wondered if he would keep his promise to come to my graduation despite our relationship status. I should not have had any expectations, and yet I was still hurt by the broken promise when he didn't show up.

To my surprise, although my ex didn't show up for graduation, Sanj came, as did some of my girlfriends. My family was also there, and everyone behaved, even my dad. The Knight family hosted a celebration lunch and an afternoon of fun and fellowship. I was surrounded by those I loved; That weekend was an opportunity to celebrate how I had loved my time at university and all the wonderful memories, growth, and self-discoveries I would always associate with that place.

That evening all my friends hung out at the Knights' house, watching a movie, relaxing, and enjoying the time we had together. We knew that goodbyes were just twelve hours away. Everyone in the group was paired off in couples, except for Sanj and me. I appreciated our friendship so much and was touched that he had made the trip to celebrate with me.

After the movie, everyone crashed in the basement family room together. Sanj and I were next to each other. I realized he was not asleep, though many of the group had dozed off during the movie.

Sanj turned to me and kissed me. I was shocked. My emotions were in one big knot, like a ball of yarn. I started laughing in the midst of the kiss.

Sanj looked at me. "That's not the reaction I was hoping for!"

I had dreamt about this moment forever, yet as it was happening it felt surreal. I replied with a giggle. "What are we doing?"

Sanj held my gaze, "I don't know, but it feels right, doesn't it?"

Morning came. At some point during the night everyone, except Linda and I who were staying there, had left to go back to wherever they were staying. When we awoke I giddily told Linda, "He kissed me!"

I will never forget her reply. "WHO?!!"

I laughed so hard! How many times had she heard me whining about Sanj? How many times had she watched me lick my wounds? Since everyone there was a couple, the answer should have been obvious, and yet the obvious was so far-fetched that her look of confusion was absolutely appropriate.

"Sanj!!!"

Her expression went from confusion, to shock, to delight.

I love that God knew what a romantic I was and gave me a delightful romance. That morning, Sanj and I went to breakfast with all my friends. As we sat beside each other, he reached for my hand under the table and held it. I will always remember the feeling of his hand as he reached for mine. He hung out with me for one more day before he had to head back to Toronto, where he was working at a hospital.

As we went our separate ways, both our minds were buzzing. He later told me that on his drive home, his mind was filled with many thoughts. We had been friends for so many years; would romance mess things up? Sanj has always been an overthinker, and he later admitted to writing a letter to tell me that it wasn't a good idea for us to date each other. Obviously, that letter was never mailed! I am so grateful that God eventually put those fears of his to rest.

I too felt a bit skittish, though my love for him outweighed my fear of being hurt again. Yet the truth was that underneath, I did not feel like a whole person.

Our courtship was not all peaches and cream. We had our ups and downs as we adjusted to learning the deeper things about each other that friendship alone could not uncover. We had to learn to accept friends and family that were in each other's world. We had to find a balance in our lives, as we were and continue to be extreme opposites in many ways. For me, at least, that led to some hurt until we were able to reach an understanding. Sanj was almost four years my senior, and I felt like I had to catch up to him. Embracing adulthood was easier for him than it was for me.

We had been friends for years before being a couple, so we knew each other far too well for pretenses. I had loved him forever; I absolutely adored him.

A month or two after we began dating, he gifted me with a locket with a little note inside it: "I ♥ U." It was such a sweet gesture and I was touched. To return the sentiment, I bought him a dozen white chocolate roses with an "I ♥ U too" card. Shortly after, he said those words aloud. My heart was full and overflowing.

Almost a year later, Sanj was home in a room he was renting and he was starving. He looked around and noticed the white chocolate roses I had given him so he began eating them to ease his hunger. Not long afterward, he called to tell me he was violently ill. The roses were obviously too old to make his stomach happy! To this day, twenty-eight years later, the sight of white chocolate still makes him sick.

For two years we dated long distance. I stayed in Michigan for a year, substitute teaching, while Sanj worked at a hospital in Toronto, seven hours away, as an audiologist. He came up on weekends, and I would hitch rides whenever I found someone heading to Toronto. We talked on the phone every day.

When I got a job teaching in a church school in Ottawa, I was grateful to be in the same country and province, even though we were still three hours apart. I taught first through third grades and lived in an apartment that, looking back, was not much better than the trailer in the cornfield in Indiana. At least there was no corn.

Most of the money I made, aside from rent, was spent on bus tickets back and forth to Toronto, and ridiculous long-distance phone bills. This was back when each long-distance call was charged by the amount of time spent on the call. My bills were easily $600 a month, a huge chunk of my paycheck. Sanj's phone bills were likely similar.

I quickly discovered that I didn't enjoy being alone. I lived for the weekends. TV was barely an option; I didn't have cable but had set up an umbrella to use as an antenna. I also missed my brothers—Rajiv had enlisted in the army, while Kumar was in Papua, New Guinea as a missionary. I missed my circle of college friends. I was lonely.

The principal and his family were lovely and kind to me; I enjoyed teaching and loved my students. My worst nightmare was dealing with the parents. The community at large seemed cold, and didn't embrace someone new, which only added to my isolation.

During those solitary evenings in my Ottawa apartment I wrote in my journal, trying to process my thoughts and confusion over this phase of life. I wrote about BR, feeling it was therapeutic to vent and express the thoughts that I couldn't verbalize to anyone. And I continued to write about our family dynamics, as I always had.

Ottawa winters proved frightening! I didn't have a vehicle and relied on the city bus for transportation. Many a time in the winter I saw buses slide onto the sidewalk due the icy streets, but nobody seemed to think much of it. Darkness came early in the winter months, and the dark and I were never friends.

I lived on the top floor of my apartment complex—where the fancy penthouse might have been in a nicer building. But my apartment was far from being a penthouse. Since the apartment was on the top floor, no one had bothered to put a lock on the sliding door that led to the balcony. I was petrified that someone would get in. I constantly imagined an intruder—or, worse, BR—finding his way in. I knew it was unlikely, but that irrational fear never went away.

The neighbors in the next apartment brought back my worst memories of home. They were a husband and wife who were physically abusive to each other. As I lay in bed listening to this couple yell, shout, and throw each other around, I relived the nightmares of home, numb with fear of what they might do to each other. One day, I met a neighbor from across the hall and mentioned the couple next to me. This neighbor told me these fights were a regular occurrence,

My mom and dad on their wedding day.
My mom's smile is forced, as just days
before she had buried her beloved father.

My first birthday.

Me at five months.

At the age of two I became
Rajiv's big sister.

Our family, complete with
the birth of Kumar.

My mom and my grandma (my dad's
mom), posing after my dad yelled at
them to stand for a picture.

Our family, shortly after moving to
Orlando. My mom made a statement
with her short hair and her choice to
wear dresses over the traditional sari.

Christmas, with the smiles and delight
that came with the season.

This was my small, sixty-pound frame when I was beat for the milk I did not spill.

Me in my late teens, feeling confident and more carefree outside the walls of high school.

This was our weekly routine—singing at various nursing homes on the weekend. Our expressions reveal our true feelings.

My high school graduation. My mom was so proud of each of our milestones.

My mom gifted my dad with a video camera. It became his constant companion.

We did not dress in our tradition Indian clothing except for random pictures.

Muhammad Ali and me!

Life at university offered a freedom I had never known.

With my family at my university graduation.

My guys who came
and celebrated my
twenty-first birthday.

The journey of finding
myself was exciting.

Reema,
meet me at
Taco Bell By the
Mall.
BR

BR made a trip to Taco Bell feel
innocent, as I loved spending
time with his son.

Sanj and me as a couple. Finally!

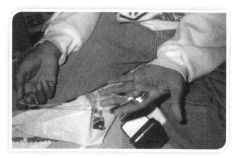

I did not understand what
was happening.

Unknown to me, the proposal.

Sanj: "Do you like it?!!"

Wood Ewe Mare-E ME?
(a picture of Sanj filled the last blank).

All is well that ends well,
with a ring on my finger!

Teaching was a fulfilling career choice for me.

Our wedding day was picture perfect.

This was the last time we were all together as a family.

Nine months pregnant and so excited to become a mom.

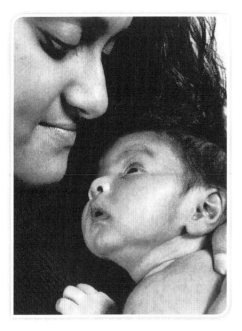 

The love of a mother for her child
is such a beautiful thing.

My mom with her first grandchild.
This look of pure happiness was
one we saw as she held each of her
thirteen grandchildren.

My boys adored their Amamma (their name for her).

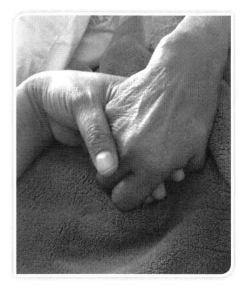

This photo was taken at my dad's funeral. We were always a unit, despite everything. There was a sense of peace in this moment.

My mom and me, both hands that had been through so much together.

I have been able to share my story and offer workshops to increase awareness on the issue of sexual abuse throughout North America.

This man has given me the freedom to be who I am meant to be and has loved me wholeheartedly.

My family. They say a picture is worth a thousand words. How blessed am I?

and when the police were called, the couple would both deny there were issues. Thinking about my dad and his treatment of my mom, I wondered if this was some people's messed up love language.

Chapter Twenty-Eight

"If you live to be a hundred, I want to live to be a hundred minus one day, so I don't have to live without you."
—A.A. Milne

By this point, Sanj and I had been dating for a year and a half. We knew we would marry someday, but it wasn't something we had talked about directly. At one point we were invited to the home of one of his friends and the question was inevitably asked: "When are you going to get married?" It was an awkward moment. While we both knew in our hearts that this was where we were heading, we had not yet had a serious conversation about marriage.

But as time moved on, engagement and marriage became part of our daily casual conversation. I was confident that Sanj would officially propose to me at Christmas. But when I hinted that I was sure of this, he insisted that wasn't the plan. Sanj was living with his brother Raj; they had purchased a house together in Scarborough, Ontario, near his work. Raj was now a police officer, and he often saved me the tortuous Greyhound journey back to Ottawa by driving me there himself and then promptly turning around and driving the three hours back. Mind you, if you knew anything about Raj's driving you would also know that the three-hour trip would have been considerably shorter for him! Raj easily became another brother to me.

I spent that Christmas with Sanj's family. It was a hard Christmas as it was the first one I had spent away from home. Christmases at home had never been very happy times, but they were all I knew. Sanj and I decided to exchange our gifts the day after Christmas, in the comfort and privacy of his home.

I loved giving gifts! Since most of my paycheck was spent on rent and my phone bill, I had little money to get Sanj the super awesome gift I wanted. My dear brother-in-law-to-be went in on the gift with me, and I was delighted to buy Sanj an awesome pair of Bauer Supreme hockey skates. These were arguably the best skates on the market at the time. They cost $500 and I was thrilled to be able to give him such an extravagant present.

Sanj was happy with the skates, but I think we both more excited about my gift, which I had not yet opened. I was sure I knew what it was going to be and had actually told my best friend that this was going to be the big day. Raj was there taking pictures, which, to me, confirmed that I was getting something special. I knew he was going to propose!

Sanj walked in carrying a huge box, awkwardly wrapped, meaning he had wrapped it himself. It was obviously *not* a jewelry box. I was disappointed, while Sanj seemed a little too thrilled.

I opened the massive box, not knowing what to expect. Inside was another wrapped box. I unwrapped that box, still hopeful. Inside the box was a rectangular piece of wood about a foot long and six inches high. My eyes rolled internally—maybe even externally. The wood had four long dashes with an E in between the last two dashes. Along with the piece of wood, there was also another, smaller box waiting to be unwrapped.

By this time, my smile had faded a bit, but Sanj was still beaming. Inside the next box was a picture of a sheep! Defeat overtook me. Obviously he was being obnoxious, and I was wrong about the proposal.

Sanj told me to place the sheep on the first dash. Then he asked me to open the next box. In the box was a horse. What was wrong with this man? I'd given him a thoughtful gift and he was giving me foolishness! What was with these farm animals? I was a bit flustered by now. Sanj was a very thoughtful man who usually showered me with thoughtful gifts, so this was all very confusing. A piece of wood, a sheep, a horse, and then the letter E on the board. I was still trying to paste a smile on my face. I mean, it really was the thought that counted right? Sanj had taken time to wrap each of the boxes in his way. Sigh.

The next box contained a picture of Sanj. That was to go on the last dash. "Do you get it!?" he asked, excitedly.

OBVIOUSLY NOT! A piece of wood, a sheep, a horse, an E, and a picture of Sanj?

Sanj is a very smart man. His mom loved to remind me that his IQ was rather high. I, on the other hand, could never focus enough to finish those standardized tests. At this point, Sanj started to help me out. He pointed out that the clues of wood, a sheep, a horse, an E, and a picture of himself, were to be read as a sequence.

"What's another name for a sheep?" he prodded, holding up the picture of the sheep.

I rolled my eyes again. This was getting frustrating.

"Ewe!" he said, supplying the answer.

I still didn't get it, even when he quizzed me on the horse. "It's a … MARE," he explained. My mind just didn't think like his (truth be told, it never has). But finally, as I looked at Sanj's own picture in the last dash, everything fell into place.

WOOD, EWE, MARE, E, ME?

My eyes lit up. I was sure I had solved the puzzle, but I didn't dare say it out loud yet. And yes, there was another box—a smaller, jewelry sized box. At last, we were getting to the point!

I opened the jewelry box with great expectation. There sat a horrifyingly ugly, gargantuan heart-shaped locket. Sanj excitedly asked, "Do you like it?"

What in the world? We had looked at rings together. He knew what I liked. Again, I paused, wondering what was wrong with this man. As I held this horrible locket in my hand, trying to figure out how to be honest, I noticed scotch tape on the side holding the locket closed. I was able to exhale. I opened the locket and there, nestled in ugliness, sat my beautiful ring.

Sanj still loves to tell this story. He brags about how he "won" by not proposing on Christmas. He still loves his proposal and the creativity of it … and I, in turn, love that he loves it.

As hard as it was to return to Ottawa and leave Sanj, it became bearable as I counted down the weeks. I spent hours planning, making creative newsletters to the bridal party, and looking for a dress. I knew I wanted a Cinderella-style romantic wedding. I wanted my Happily Ever After.

Chapter Twenty-Nine

"Life continues, and we all of us keep changing and building, toward what we cannot know."

—Lois Duncan

Around the time that I got engaged, my parents moved to Texas, where my mom got a job. In the spring of that year, Sanj and I made a trip to visit my parents there. I had not seen my parents or brothers in more than a year, and I looked forward to eating my mom's food. Kumar was still in New Guinea but Rajiv was home. I had never been to this house, or to Texas, for that matter. I was so happy to make the 24-hour road trip with Sanj and escape from my "penthouse" apartment.

When we passed through Dayton, we stopped to see a friend of ours who was still in high school there. It was the day before Youth Rally weekend and the school was buzzing. As I walked in through the main doors, walking out of the gym directly in front of me was BR and his wife.

I probably should have been prepared to run into him, but I wasn't. I knew by then that they'd had a second child and, doing the math, I realized that shortly after he raped me, she became pregnant. He had used no protection when he brutally forced himself into me. That could have been me!

BR acted happy to see me, greeting me with a hug. I wondered if he could feel my shaking body. His wife followed with a hug too. I felt sick to my stomach, feeling as if I had betrayed her. I also felt so sad for her and pitied her lack of awareness as to whom she has married.

From there, we went on to Texas, where we visited my parents.

It had been more than a year since I had last seen them, and the dynamic between my parents seemed different.

I thought back to the allegation my parents' employee had made about my dad years earlier. Since then, some of my friends had told me stories of parental infidelity, usually about their fathers having affairs with other women, cheating on their mothers. Those stories made me pause and think about my dad. The incident with their employee made me realize that it was possible—perhaps even likely—that my dad had been unfaithful to my mom. But this wasn't something I could prove.

Why was I not angrier about that? Perhaps because my mom had seemed to brush off the allegations against my dad, it was easier for us kids to just brush it off too. Now, as I observed the new dynamic between my parents, I was clueless as to what caused the change, but my mom seemed to have gained a backbone and my dad seemed to have been put in his place. She now took charge of the finances, managed the household, and kept control of the money. She changed her attitude toward him as well, treating him with blatant disdain.

I found the whole change in their dynamic disturbing. My mom had always been too kindhearted to treat my dad the way he deserved. Now it turned my stomach to watch this messy cat and mouse game playing out between them. Why didn't they just get a divorce? Over the years, my mom had always told us she had stayed with him for our sake. Once we had all moved out of the house her reason for staying with him seemed to change to: "If I left him, what would happen to him?"

CHAPTER THIRTY

*"Bravery is the capacity to perform properly
even when scared half to death."*
—Omar N. Bradley

In March, Sanj and I chose the pastor that we wanted to marry us. We didn't know him well, but he was one of the pastors at the church we attended. He was also of Indian heritage and our families knew his family, so there was an immediate connection. We went weekly to marriage counseling, as was highly recommended by those we respected. Pagie, our pastor, did many things that I assumed were typical of marriage counseling. We had homework and were encouraged to think outside the box, often bringing up issues that we might never have thought of before marriage.

Sanj knew about my rape before we started dating, but only in vague terms. As we dated and I talked about it further, we found ourselves in foreign territory. It was one of the things that caused unrest between us. We learned that BR had been invited to speak at the high school from which Sanj had graduated. Knowing he was so close to us geographically was stressful. Sanj wanted to cause BR bodily harm, while I just wanted it to all go away. We decided that we would take this to Pagie, our counselor.

After I shared the whole painful story, Pagie looked at me and said, "Reema, you have to do something." He pointed out that if BR was sorry, he would have let me know. I realized this was something I would have to deal with before I could move on.

Pagie told me that if I was willing, we would do this together, but still I was scared. I was twenty-five years old, in a country where my fiancé was my only support. All the other people who might support me were in the States.

By contrast, BR had simply continued on with life as he knew it, confident that I posed no threat to him. He and his wife now had a second child; he lived and worked in a place where people worshiped the ground he walked on. How was I going to go up against this beloved pastor, husband, and father who had all the love and support he could wish for? Who would believe my word against his?

I was to learn that when God calls you, He will empower you. Pagie asked me to call BR and tape a conversation where I would tell him in no uncertain terms that he raped me, and we would take it from there.

Twice before, I had made an effort to address what had happened with BR. I had spoken to him directly the year before, on a visit to my parents when they were still in Dayton. When I told BR he had taken advantage of me, he told me that he felt that in a way *he* had been taken advantage of too! He took no responsibility for raping me. I had also written him a letter expressing my anger, after my brief encounter with him on our trip down to Texas, but he had not replied. Now to follow up by confronting him directly over the phone would be one of the hardest things I had ever had to do.

I chose to make the call alone because I did not want to put Sanj through the pain of listening to the conversation. Leaving him in Toronto, I returning to Ottawa. I was alone in my apartment, petrified. How was I going to say, "You raped me!"? How could I get through this conversation, knowing that I needed to record it so that BR wouldn't be able to do to others what he'd done to me? I sat on my bed, the only piece of furniture in my penthouse, and practiced recording with the tape recorder on the phone.

On March 22, 1994, three months before my wedding, I called my rapist. My heart was pounding, my hands shaking. I am not sure how I spoke at all except God gave me the strength.

The first minute was an uncomfortable greeting, and then his son interrupted. BR told him to go take his bath (ironically, where his son had been when BR raped me). After some small talk, I brought up what I really wanted to say. This is a transcript of that phone call:

Me: *I am getting married in a few weeks. I am so grateful that God has answered my prayers and blessed me with an amazing guy. As I mentioned in my letter, I was very angry that you took my virginity away without my consent and that really hurt a lot. I was confused about all that happened, and then what happened with LB.*

(LB was our family friend to whom BR had made inappropriate comments at around the same time he raped me. I knew that since my brother had confronted him about that incident, BR would be thinking of it, along with what he had done to me).

You told me how special I was and how much you loved me. I had no idea what was happening. When I came home to do my student teaching, you befriended me. I thought you were safe. You were a pastor. You were married. You were a father. I trusted you. You made me trust you. I shared with you my broken heart. I trusted you.

I told you that I had lost my virginity to you without my consent. I told you in my letter that you raped me. I told you I had been taken advantage of and you told me that you felt like you had been taken advantage of too! What?!!!

You said that I was too immature to handle this "relationship." I hope I am never mature enough to handle a relationship forced upon me, based on lies. You really don't know how much pain you caused, maybe you can hear it in my voice. I gave you my trust, when I had nothing else to give, and all I wanted back was a friendship. You were someone I should have been able to trust to be my friend! You took something away from me that I will never get back. Why ME? Can you answer any of this?

I went on to say that he knew I was emotionally fragile and had been aware of my wounds. I told him that he had betrayed my trust and stolen something that I would never get back.

This was his reply:

BR: *Well, there's a couple of things, I wanted to hear you out. I didn't want to interrupt. There are a couple of things I feel the need to say. I kind of hesitate to say much as I don't want anything to be misconstrued. And you are right, it is hard to know how another person feels. You just said a moment ago you wish I knew how you felt. And you recognize it's difficult to understand what another is experiencing. And so I don't want to say anything that would be taken the wrong way, and not taken the way I meant it. I'm very hesitant to say anything. One of my biggest regrets is the fact that you know when you have a precious friendship, and to lose it is very detrimental. I don't think it was either of our intentions to cross any lines or to go any further than the type of friendship we had. I think it is the nature of the beast, nature of sin that causes one to go beyond even though your intentions are good.*

No matter how good you are, or how good you try to be, or your intentions are, it's not very hard to fall down. And it's not very hard to go down fast. I think LB understands now that whole episode was extremely innocent, and nothing was intended or like that. I think the Lord allowed that whole experience (with that student) to happen for me to see something else.

And I have thought about you, cried about you and I've prayed for you. And the main reason is you are a very precious person. I know that you would give your life to help and bless other people. And just the thought that you felt betrayed and/or taken advantage of was crushing. And no, I can't begin to know how you feel but I can sense to some degree the pain. And all I can do is try and understand you and allow you like when you vented in your letter and so forth. I mean I knew you had to do that, you had to get it out, it was eating you up. I tried not to take it all personally, you know cause …

Me: *Do you not take any responsibility?*

BR: *No, that's not what I am saying. I am not saying that at all. See, that's why I hesitate to say anything because I don't want you to think I'm shucking anything, turning my back on anything.*

Me: *BR, I guess that's what I wanted to know, because you remember when I came home shortly after I started dating Sanj, and we met? I told you that you that you had taken my virginity away and that was really hard for me, to stand up and say that. And I just felt like it was no big deal to you. That you were blaming me for everything. That really hurt a lot.*

I came to tell you that you took something very special away from me. The hardest thing now is knowing I am getting married and knowing I am not going to give that to Sanj, that hurts so much. He is the one that deserves it. He loves me so much and he has been by my side through thick and thin. I don't know, I guess I wanted to hear you say that YOU ARE SORRY! Yet you didn't. Do you understand?

BR: *I understand. I understand exactly what you're saying now. I don't know if you think that I'm experienced at handling perfectly every situation that comes my way. I was not prepared to deal with our conversation that day and I probably....*

Me: *But that's why I came to you out of the blue, because I didn't want a rehearsed speech.*

BR: *Just because someone knows something doesn't mean you're going to get a rehearsed speech. I mean I knew you were going to call tonight, and I didn't prepare something. It's just that you take any situation, particularly when a person is wounded or hurt, umm, they are much more sensitive than they normally are when they are wounded or hurt. I wish I did know all the right things to say or the right way to respond and I was wrong for my reaction, and one of those things I would like you to understand is that I am and still am. That why I say I pray for you. I don't think of you with disdain and still think very highly of you. I know things will never be the same, but I still think of you as one of the best friends I have had.*

I guess a part of the whole situation was that I had, and it's not your fault, it's my fault, that I had reached a place in my experience where I just lived so secluded trying to be, you know, Mr. Everything to everyone in terms of the school. I didn't take any time for myself and my own life. Then I met you and a friendship blossomed, a very pure and innocent friendship. And then all of a sudden, I am finding that I am taking time just for me and this is a good thing. I finally have a friend just for the sake of me and had nothing to do with anybody else and I think my own selfishness kicked in and the process, umm, you were wounded and that was something that—looking back, that's my biggest regret.

You know when you have something or someone that's precious to you, you don't want to do anything that would wound or hurt them. Yeah I take all the responsibility.

You may think, the things I've said, that I'm trying to place blame somewhere and I am really not.

And my main regret is that I once had a very dear precious friend who was a genuine and true friend who was not in it for anything, just because of her kindhearted nature and through a series of events that friendship will no longer be like it was.

This was the gist of the conversation. I never received an apology; three decades later, that has still never happened.

While we were talking, his doorbell rang. Students had come over to hang out. He took the call upstairs. He went on to tell me that he had resigned, and that he and his family were moving south to be near relatives. Again, at this point, he seemed to draw me into the conversation as if we were friends.

After the phone call, I felt a sense of pride that I had found the strength to accomplish this task. Yet at the same time, so many emotions flooded through me, confusion being the primary one.

As I look back at this transcript it's obvious that BR was still playing a role, trying to manipulate me during the conversation. He was trying to be dominant in his role as a counselor, not the perpetrator that he was. He was trying to validate and perpetuate the lie about what had happened, trying to portray what happened between us as a "relationship" rather than the vile and, as he put it, "selfish act" that it was.

There were only eight weeks until my wedding day! It was such an exciting time, and I could not wait to be Mrs. Reema Sukumaran. But along with the excitement came anxiety and stress. I was so afraid something would go wrong. Life with my family seemed to be like a powder keg that could blow up at any time and usually at the worst time. Meanwhile, I was still dealing with the aftermath of having confronted BR.

Everything happened quickly, like falling dominos. Pagie contacted the principal of the school where BR worked and informed him about many details of my case. This was the same principal who had been in charge when my brothers and I were students. I wonder how he lived with the fact that he had let us down when we were younger. He was a mandatory reporter who was legally obligated to report the abuse we were living with at home but did not. The abuse we were living with was no secret. I wonder how many knew and turned a blind eye. The principal knew. The bottom line is HE DID NOT CARE.

I already distrusted this principal because of his failure to help us when we were young people living in an abusive situation. I also knew the he was best buds with BR, and unlikely to take any action. In every situation, he chose to look the other way. It was apparent that he really did not have the best interest of the students in mind.

I was not the only girl that BR was sexually inappropriate with, and the principal had been told about at least one other situation—the girl who BR had kissed in his office. Nothing had happened then, even when the girl and her aunt brought the matter to the principal; no one wanted to disturb the status quo. It was the principal's responsibility to hold BR accountable, but he preferred to sweep these allegations under the rug.

This was why it had been so important for me to record the phone call with BR. No one would do anything unless there was leverage to bring about action. Nothing happened until Pagie made a phone call to the principal and made it clear that action had to be taken, and that we had a recording to further substantiate this claim of rape. He told the principal that if action wasn't taken by the employer, then legal action would be our only remaining choice.

Our request was that BR be fired from his position as chaplain, and banned from working in the church, particularly from working with young people or children. He was also to stay away from me, an informal restraining order of sorts.

On May 24, 1994—five weeks before my wedding—BR was called into the principal's office. He denied the allegation immediately, until they informed him about the tape. As soon he was notified about the tape the denials stopped. His only question was: What did we want? He was fired immediately, told to turn in his ministerial license, and ordered not to have contact with me.

As BR closed up shop, he was given permission to write the school community a letter. In the letter he told his version of the story: how during a low period in his life, after his mother's death, a young lady had come into his life and taken advantage of him. He had messed up and was now dealing with the consequences of these actions. Even in leaving, he was allowed to control the narrative instead of owning the truth. The principal even wrote BR a glowing recommendation.

As soon as BR was let go, the rumors started. Some were close to the truth—many people in the community were saying that BR had raped someone. Within a week, my name was out, but most people heard that it was a consensual affair.

Reading through my journals now, I see how much heartache I experienced while all this was unfolding. I felt deeply for his wife, who apparently left him. I respected her for taking this action. I hated knowing that he would lie to her and that she would probably believe I had betrayed her. I filled up pages of my journal beseeching God to pour strength into my weary body.

I came out with my story in large part because I could not live with myself knowing that he might do the same thing to someone else. My will to protect others came with a price. I discovered what a boys' club the church was. BR was "dealt with." We had asked that he turn in his ministerial license; we assumed that would bar him from the pulpit and keep him away from having access to vulnerable young people. Being so young and naive, I trusted that things would be done in everyone's best interest, mine included.

Though I heard nothing immediately about what happened to BR, I later learned that he had moved away but continued working in a position that allowed him access to vulnerable people. Nothing had really changed.

I had been part of this church since I was born. My grandfather had been a minister in this organization. But my church had failed me. The attitude in those days was to simply move your problem away, allowing it to become someone else's problem. The sad reality is that this was how many organizations functioned at that time.

CHAPTER THIRTY-ONE

*"Once in a while, right in the middle of an ordinary life,
love gives us a fairy tale."*
—Unknown

The weekend of July 3, 1994 finally arrived. I was flooded with so many emotions. I was finally going to be with my family again. Rajiv was driving from Dayton, Ohio where he had been working that summer. My parents were coming from Texas, as was Kumar, who had just returned from his year in Papua, New Guinea. Rajiv and my parents were stuck across the border for a day, something about paperwork for my grandmother, who was also with them. Drama of some sort seemed to always follow them.

Sanj and I went to pick up Kumar from the border, as I was eager to see him again after his year in New Guinea. For some reason, the border patrol chose to give us a hard time. Because we had crossed the border for less than twenty-four hours, they refused to believe we hadn't purchased anything, since many people from Canada went to the US for cross-border shopping. They made us pull into the area where they searched our car and opened my brother's suitcase. They had caught us red handed—or so they thought.

Kumar shared some of my dad's OCD tendencies: he was obsessed with order and had to have everything organized. The border guards opened his suitcase to find it packed immaculately. His clothes were pressed, starched, and folded with such precision that they did look new. His watch was even in a case, and we had to point out that the watch case and watch were not even the same brand! They still gave us a hard time and said we were required to pay $50 for duty. Instead, we chose to take the suitcase back for my parents to bring across when they came the next day.

My heart was full as the people dearest to me arrived for my wedding. Sanj and I had limited funds, and we were paying for the wedding ourselves, so we chose to focus on the ceremony, hoping to make it meaningful to us but also something that others would enjoy and remember. Sanj, being a musician who had worked with many other musicians, called in all his favors and had a beautiful lineup of music. My dress was my one splurge item, as I had it custom designed and made. It was all I had hoped for, and I felt like a princess.

I had eight of my dearest friends stand up for me, Linda being my maid of honor. Sanj had eight groomsmen; his brother was his best man. My brothers read 1 Corinthians 13, the "Love Chapter," from the Bible. Adding to the wedding procession were many children. Jonathan and Jessica were candle bearers, ending with the Bible boy and a delightful miniature bride and groom—the children of friends of ours—to complete the wedding party.

I waited with breathless anticipation as the processional for the bridal party played and our friends walked down the aisle, each of the girls looking beautiful in her red bridesmaid's dress. As the pipe organ crescendoed into Mendelssohn's "Wedding March," I took my dad's arm. The doors opened, and down that aisle was my incredible gift from God, looking so handsome in his tuxedo. His eyes held mine as I walked toward him. I watched as he dabbed his eyes, knowing without a doubt that he was the best thing. He loved me.

We reached the end of the aisle. I kissed my dad's cheek, looked into his eyes, and said, "Daddy, I love you." Maybe it was manipulative of me, but I wanted, needed him to say it … those three words as I left his home. Of course he would say, "I love you too."

My dad, without missing a beat, replied, "Thank you."

Chapter Thirty-Two

"The power and intensity of your contractions cannot be stronger than you, because it is you."
—Unknown

Saying goodbye to all our friends and family who had come for our wedding was hard, but I was excited to start life as Mrs. Sukumaran.

I moved in with Sanj and his brother in the house they had purchased together the year before. The three of us settled into a comfortable rhythm. We didn't have the traditional honeymoon period, but it seemed to work for us. I didn't have a job, apart from the occasional call to substitute teach. Both of us were eager to start our family and, since I was at home anyway, we saw no reason to wait.

Three months after saying "I do," I was carrying a new life in me. We were beyond thrilled! I had the typical morning sickness that soon turned into regurgitating whatever I had just inhaled within minutes. Despite my nausea, I knew the baby was healthy, and I loved everything else about being pregnant. I couldn't wait to have my belly show, to wear maternity clothes, and to have everyone know I was pregnant. I was so ready to be a mom.

Adjusting to life in this new place was harder than I thought. Though I enjoyed being married, in other ways I was as lonely as I had been in Ottawa. I had no real friends nearby. Letter writing was my primary means of communication at that time; the price of long distance calling always made me pause. I missed my tribe. Sanj's world had not changed; he still had his sports, his music, and his friends. Nothing had changed in his world except the addition of love.

My parents came to visit as my due date approached and then passed. The little one showed no signs of making an appearance. I was impatient. It was summer, and I was hot and uncomfortable with my pregnant belly, swollen legs, and huge breasts. I was miserable and scared, but I was ready.

I felt a tightening, a wave of something twisting, pulling, and squeezing my insides. If I fought it, it fought back! While my stomach caused me agony, my back seemed to be throwing its own temper tantrum. No one warned me about *this*! I mean, we went to all those prenatal classes. What was wrong with my back? The pain in my back was almost worse than what my belly was doing.

We lived about a city block away from the hospital and arrived at a maternity ward that was overcrowded that night, with eight ladies in active labor! I will always be grateful that we had a room, which gave us some privacy. Well, sort of. The whole family was there, in my room, watching this freak show. Yes, all of them. My in-laws, my mom and dad, even a cousin of Sanj's. Everyone was excited for this baby!

I was uncomfortable. Sanj's touch, normally so comforting, was an irritant, and yet I desperately wanted his comfort. In the midst of all of this discomfort and pain, I lay there wondering when this hell I was in would end. Would death be better? I held my breath as the contraction that tormented my body did its thing. As I had mentioned, we had gone to prenatal classes and Lamaze training. Sanj, ever the logical thinker, suggested I use the breathing techniques we had learned and practiced in Lamaze class. So, I began: "Ha, Ha, Hee! Ha, Ha, Hee!"

He stopped me.

"You're not doing it right! It's HEE, HEE, HA, not HA, HA, HEE," he corrected me.

I was in the worst pain I had ever been in and this crazy man was correcting my breathing! Amazingly, he lived. It's a favorite story that has been retold over the years.

One of our dear friends, Sharon, was a nurse at the hospital. She popped in to see how I was doing and was appalled to see the room full of family. I will never forget the moment she looked at me, saw my consternation, and firmly told them all to GET OUT! I will be forever grateful. I only wanted my mom and husband there. I wanted to suffer in private.

Everyone has their labor story, as did I, and twelve hours later this gunky blob of flesh was put in my arms. I was appalled at how unattractive this baby was in that first moment, after all that work. Still, we had a son! A beautiful son, as it turned out. Amazing what a transformation a little wash could accomplish. He was perfect; he was absolutely precious! It was love at first sight. My heart overflowed with gratitude as I became a mom. Despite all the ongoing pain I was still experiencing, my heart felt nothing except love. Love like I had never felt before.

Samuel Peter (named after both grandfathers, and another attempt to show my dad that I yearned for him in my life) was showered with constant love and affection from everyone in his life. It was hard for me to share him. He was such a happy baby and just so gorgeous. Did others have babies this beautiful? Quietly I doubted that anyone had ever had a more beautiful baby.

My mom and dad stayed for a few weeks. I was sore and found it hard to be still and let my body take the time to heal. Aside from Sanj and my mom, I didn't trust anyone else with my baby. I was grateful for all the help that came with my mom's visit.

CHAPTER THIRTY-THREE

"It hurts to let go, but sometimes it hurts more to hold on."
—Unknown

My parents left. I was glad they had come for my son's birth, but it was hard for me to accept that my mom's life had not really changed. Despite some superficial changes in the dynamic between my parents, she was still living as a battered woman. I resented her for staying with my dad for all these years—especially since she had claimed for so long that she was staying for the sake of her children.

My parents had moved around a lot after leaving Ohio. They sold their elder care business, for reasons unknown to us until later. At some point while in Texas, things were bad enough that they were about to be homeless. Not long after our son Sammy was born, Sanj, being the generous person he is, offered to have them come and live with us until they could figure things out. They were Canadian citizens, so moving back was not a problem. The plan was that they would move to Toronto and stay with us while my mom looked for a job and they were able to get situated again.

Sammy's first Christmas had arrived! I was so excited to finally have the Christmas I had always dreamed of. We had a tree full of decorations, with beautiful matching colored lights strung here, there, and everywhere. The tree had gifts surrounding it to a maximum capacity, and then some. It was picture perfect! Kind of like a Norman Rockwell painting—but with brown people.

That Christmas was important to me. Now that I was married and had a child, I had promised myself that my family would always know Christmas as Christmas was supposed to be. It would be full of the traditional decorations, a real tree, lots of lights inside and out. We would make our own traditions and be the family that I had always wished for. I told myself that my dad didn't have any power over me anymore. I was sure that it would be easy to move forward.

On Christmas morning, while everyone was sound asleep, there was a knock on our bedroom door. It wasn't even five o'clock. My mom was at our door, telling us that my dad was leaving.

Of course he was! Of course he would find a way to mess up Sammy's first Christmas, just as he had ruined ours over and over again! I didn't know what had happened to trigger this; I just knew that I was incensed and I no longer cared. Whatever the reason, he could have waited until this day was over. There was no excuse for his behavior. It was unforgivable. I told my mom, "Let him go."

Some things never change. My dad had ruined my perfect Christmas. Again. Our one family Christmas tradition was having our dad leave us on Christmas, and now he had done it again.

All I knew at the time was that my parents had had a fight. Who knows what they fought about? My dad struggled with living under our roof. He wasn't in control in our house, and he was scared of Sanj.

That Christmas morning marked a turning point. "If you leave him," we told my mom, "you can live with us. You can relax, retire, and enjoy your grandbaby."

That was the day my mom finally left my dad—or perhaps, more accurately, it was the day we took her from him. She couldn't do it herself. Truth be told, it was Sammy who liberated my mom, as her love for him seemed to overpower all else. Sammy was the deal breaker.

My dad used that fight Christmas morning to leave us permanently. He left before we woke up, to save face, more than likely. He took a bus and moved back to Tennessee where they had lived for a short period of time.

Our family grew quickly after that first Christmas, and before long we had six boys! In the years that followed, our family Christmases were just what you might imagine with six boys. There was always a lot of noise, excitement, wrapping paper everywhere, food, fun, and as little drama as possible.

A few years ago, our whole family was together, my dad included, with my in-laws and extended family for Christmas at our house. It was just what I had always wanted for Christmas! While it was all good, I felt something that I could not explain. I was so worried about what might happen. How would my dad disrupt Christmas? He did a good job of blending into the background, hiding behind his camera. Yet the fear of his potential disruptive behavior lingered. It was not until our Christmas celebration was over that I was able to exhale.

My dad had consistently robbed our family of the joy of Christmas when we were growing up. So even now, there's a part of me, that hidden under my smile and delight, always feels a pain and sadness.

I will always miss my dad at Christmas. Not the dad who I actually had for most of my life, but the daddy who could have delighted in Christmas. My daddy who loved me enough to want to see me happy even at the smallest of gifts. My daddy who delighted in my eyes shining as I laughed with joy at the Christmas lights. The daddy I wished for. Every year, I have to fight off the negative memories of childhood Christmases, and I am intentional in doing everything I can to make it a joyful time for my boys. I love that they ask which brother they are buying for, as we pick names. I am overjoyed knowing that this is a tradition they will continue. We always give them pajamas on Christmas Eve and as much as they groan about it, they love it.

I want my boys to know the magic that comes with Christmas. I am so glad they will never know how blessed they are to have Christmas as they know it. They will always know the magic of Christmas as part of our family experience—a family that is all together. The magic of Christmas is not really the tree, nor the beautiful lights; it's not the turkey dinner, nor the many presents. It took me a long time to understand that the real magic of Christmas—the magic I'd missed out on as a child, that I've tried to pass on to my own children—was, and is, just being together.

Sanj and I had our babies back to back. I wanted my children to be close in age, with the hopes that this would foster a close friendship between them. I never wanted any of my kids to ever be a parentified child for any reason. I will always be grateful that God blessed me with this amazing husband who was not only loving, kind, and compassionate, but who shared my dreams for our family and children.

Matthew Tyler was born two weeks after Sammy's first birthday. Jordan Michael was born sixteen months after Tyler. Having my mom there made life with three babies easier, allowing for Sanj and I to have some time alone. Life was busy and full, but above all, it was satisfying.

Every summer, my mom would go to visit my brothers for a week or so. During one of these breaks, a few months after Jordan was born, I invited my dad to visit. Despite everything, I still yearned for my dad to be my dad. I wanted him to love my boys. I was still looking to be daddy's girl.

By this time my dad had three grandsons to visit, and I went out of my way to arrange things so he could spend time with them. I was eager for him to come; I wanted him to be a part of our lives. When I called to invite him, his response was, "What will I do there?"

I was shocked and hurt by those words. I put my feelings aside, and he did come. But in the time he spent with us, his question rang true. It became obvious that he had no connection to the boys and didn't really seem to want one. He chose to leave early.

After all the hurtful things my dad had done when I was growing up, it was amazing to realize how much his words and actions still had the power to hurt me. His indifference toward my sons cut me to the quick. I had three beautiful sons that he didn't know. How could he ask what he would do here? How could he not just love them?

I was furious that this man did not understand that he was being given a gift. A relationship with his grandsons was not a right—it was a gift! A gift that in that moment was rescinded. I sat at the computer and wrote my dad an ugly but honest letter. All my hurt, anger, disappointment, and pain spewed out onto the pages. I threw his words back at him and suggested that maybe he needed to "catch his ears and say he was sorry"—a weird directive he used to give us as children that never made sense. I told him that I was his daughter and I had his temper. He just lost his chance to be in my boys' lives. I would not stand by and tolerate him hurting them. He was not allowed in their lives and that way they would never have to question his love. He was dead to me. He was done hurting me. I was taking that power away from him.

In that moment, I felt free. This man who had caused so much hurt and pain was gone. I was safe; my kids were safe; his ability to hurt me was neutralized. I had found a way to protect my family from my dad's unpredictability. A piece of me died when I wrote that letter—the part of me that had yearned for a relationship with my dad for so long—but I was also filled with a sense of relief. Having my dad in my life would only lead to more disappointment and pain. My children did not know him, and as they grew up I was very honest with them about why.

One day I would be able to see my dad more clearly and understand that much of what I despised in him was the effect of his unchecked and untreated mental illness, but at that time, all I felt was rage, pain, and relief.

HEALING

CHAPTER THIRTY-FOUR

"Don't try to understand everything, because sometimes it is not meant to be understood, but to be accepted."

—Unknown

Having my mom living with us was great; I felt like I could bless her with the life she had never had. She adored her grandchildren and they loved her back. But as much as I loved her, I found that the anger toward her that I had suppressed over the years was still there, simmering under the surface.

How had my mom allowed her children to live in such ugliness? I looked at my one-year-old baby and I couldn't imagine letting anyone hit him on the head with their knuckles. I looked at my five-year-old and I could not imagine making him do the laundry. Motherhood changed me; it gave me a new perspective and made me a fierce defender of my children.

Again and again I asked her the question: "Why did you stay with him?" It made no sense to me. She made all the money. She could have continued to live and provided for us without him. Her answer had always been consistent. She stayed with him for us. She never wanted us to resent her for leaving him, but the irony was that I resented her for staying.

Years later, my mom finally admitted that she had also worried about what her friends and family would think had she left my dad. Those fears were not unfounded; it was something she actually faced when she finally did leave my dad. Family and friends gossiped and said hurtful things, often behind her back, that caused her to withdraw from certain circles. My dad spread his version of the truth—his lies— and many people chose to believe him.

Even after she left him, my dad's vindictive behavior still cast a shadow over her life. He pressured her not to divorce him because divorce was against biblical principles. He accused her of staying with us because she was having an affair with my husband and asked if I knew what was happening under my own roof. This was the delusional nature of my dad's mental illness. I am still not sure if he was simply manipulative or if he actually believed his own lies.

The years passed and my mom continued to live with us. She was a part of our family in every sense. As much as I wanted to share with her the life that God had blessed me with, my mixed emotions grew stronger. I was furious with my mom. I couldn't articulate these emotions, but they were very real. I loved her and I resented her. My mom did not protect me as I was growing up, and now she was living my life. After all these years I allowed myself to feel the anger that grew out of being a parentified child my whole life.

Counseling to work through these issues would have been so beneficial. At times I did seek out help, but the therapists and I did not connect, making the experience frustrating and unfulfilling. Money was also an issue; insurance only covered a certain amount, so after a few sessions, our coverage was finished. I never had enough time or the right therapist to help me deal with my anger.

I often thought back to the time when my mom returned to my dad after he beat her, the time my brother and I picked up and went to Maryland with her. When that happened, I was devastated and furious, and told her that if she went back to him, she was choosing him over us, her kids. I didn't understand the hold my dad had on her, but I knew something in me hardened when she went back to him. I found myself needing to protect my heart.

Now, all these years later, when she had finally left him and was living with me, her touch was an irritant that I could not explain and my reaction was a need to withdraw. She had never been physically affectionate with us. I was a mom who loved and held my children, physically bonding to them, but as time went by, I became even less tolerant of my own mom's touch. I found myself withdrawing from it, then feeling guilty for doing so.

My boys loved their grandmother, and I was grateful that they could love her with their whole being. The bond the boys shared with my mom remained strong until her dying day. They often slept with her, pushing her to the edge of the bed right up until her life's end, despite my youngest being a man-sized child and the oldest ones actually being grown men by that time.

I had to work it out. Why did my mom's touch not give me comfort? I never doubted my mom's love for a moment. She had spent her life showing her love in her language, through acts of kindness. My mom spent more hours than most people I knew working. She cooked and made sure we had the best of meals despite her exhaustion. I knew that she would do whatever she was able to do to protect me and my brothers, often taking a beating for us, but it was not enough. I had never felt safe as a child and young adult. What I had needed was the freedom to be a child, to be safe with my family.

Instead I had learned early on that touch was not safe. My dad's touch had been violent; my pastor's touch had been violating; even an "uncle" had taught me that touch could be inappropriate and unsafe. Yet through it all, touch was still my love language. But my mom's touch seemed empty and meaningless. It left me yearning for something I was not able to describe or understand.

My mom lived with our family for five years. During these five years, she was part of our lives completely. I loved that my boys had this time with their Amamma and developed a very special bond with her. But after five years, I realized that I needed my space. I wished I didn't feel that way, but I did. In order to have a relationship with her, I needed to have some physical distance between us. Sanj and I talked about getting my Mom an apartment. I dreaded the conversation as I knew it would hurt her, and I did not want to inflict more pain.

At the time, my brother Kumar was attending school in Maryland, where my mom's family lived. Her own mother had been diagnosed with Alzheimer's and was in need of care, so my mom made the decision to move to Maryland. I liked to think that leaving my dad and living with us allowed her to develop some confidence. Or maybe I only thought this to make myself feel better.

Over the years, I became very proud of my mom and the life she made for herself. She became very self-sufficient. She found jobs as caretaker to people who needed home care. She learned to use the transit system and developed true independence. She became active in her church, took computer classes, and had her own place to decorate as she pleased.

My mom was unselfish, often lending a hand to those who needed it. She was a constant giver. She not only took care of her mom, finding a facility where my grandma was well taken care of, but moved into the apartment complex next to her. She took care of her mother and advocated for her until my grandmother passed away.

My mom found herself at age sixty-five, after she was freed from the hold my dad had on her. She continued to read as much as she wanted, watch Indian movies, complete puzzles, and spend time with her siblings. She was active in her church, often volunteering in the nursery as well as other areas in the church. We teased her about all the things she carried in her large, heavy purse. She carried treats for children and loved to give an exhausted parent a break by occupying their child with her knickknacks.

At the age of seventy-five, my mom joined the Pathfinder Club and earned her Master Guide. Pathfinders is like Boy Scouts and Girl Scouts combined. In order to achieve the highest rank of Master Guide candidates are required to complete the preceding stages and collect the badges for each stage. Much of this is based on outdoor activities, and those who gain this rank are typically young adults. My mom had this achievement on her bucket list, and she may very well have been the oldest person to complete the requirements. She had her investiture ceremony at a nationwide camporee in Oshkosh, Wisconsin, and couldn't have been happier.

In later years my mom was also quite attached to her iPad, playing games with her grandkids and texting them to stay in touch. She prayed for each of us, as well as each of her grandchildren; her greatest wish was to see us each in heaven. If we had something big or small, we could ask my mom to pray and her prayers seemed to be answered! She was indeed a prayer warrior.

Even when my mom and dad were physically apart, she was still emotionally connected to him in a way that I found hard to understand. They talked on the phone most days. On a few occasions, she even traveled to take care of him after an illness. In some way they did love each other, or perhaps were inexorably linked. It was just that their link was so dangerous because of my dad's unpredictable nature.

When I asked her in later years why she still engaged with him, I don't think she herself really understood. She would sometimes say: "If I don't care for him, who would?"

Over the years, I came to understand my mom's relationship with my dad a little better after I learned about trauma bonding, a bond that develops between victims and their abusers.

"A trauma bond is a bond that forms due to intense, emotional experiences, usually with a toxic person. It holds us emotionally captive to a manipulator who keeps us 'hostage'—whether that be through physical or emotional abuse.[1]"

CHAPTER THIRTY-FIVE

"Sometimes it's OK if the only thing you did today was breathe."
—Unknown

Sanj and I were blessed to have no problem getting pregnant. We loved our boys, who were easygoing, adorable, and fun. I loved babies. A few months or a year after having each new baby, I would look at Sanj and say, "Can we have another one? Can we try again, see if we get a girl?" This beautiful human being I am blessed to call my husband never said no to me. So, we had another baby and another until we arrived at our final total of six boys.

Max, my fourth baby, was born. He was beautiful and such an easy baby. He loved his brothers and lit up the room with his toothless grin. We were so blessed. And yet I felt a little funny. I was sad at times, instead of being elated by new parenthood as I had been with the first three. I found myself hiding around a corner or in a bedroom, crying, then pretending everything was OK. I couldn't understand it. While

[1]   https://thoughtcatalog.com/shahida-arabi/2018/04/5-signs-youre-in-a-destructive-trauma-bond-with-a-toxic-person

my life wasn't perfect, I loved it and I was happy with my husband and sons. So why was I crying and feeling this sadness?

Watching Oprah Winfrey one afternoon as she interviewed Marie Osmond, I realized that what was being described was something I was going through. Yes, once again it was Oprah who helped me recognize something I didn't fully understand: postpartum blues. I had the blues. Hormones. I told myself that it was OK; the problem would fix itself.

My fifth baby, Zachary, came two years later. As with all my babies he was beautiful, easygoing, and doted on by his brothers. The older boys loved babies. My mom came to visit and give me a hand after coming home. She would stay a month, loving on the children, cooking up a storm, and tackling the endless mounds of laundry.

Once again, I was feeling something horrible, and it wasn't just "the blues." If I had to pick a color, it would have been the blackest of blacks. I hated how low I felt. What if I was not able to find myself again? I was frightened. I felt like I could have hurt someone or something.

The moment I knew I needed help was one morning when Sanj and the boys were heading out the door for school and work. One of the boys was not listening to me about getting their socks and shoes on. I stood at the top of the stairs, screaming and yelling in frustration. They all stared at me, Sanj included, looking shocked and scared.

"What are you staring at?!?!" I screamed. "Yes, I am crazy!!"

I cried my eyes out, feeling frightened and lost. I was losing myself. I had no idea what was wrong with me. I knew then that I needed help, but I still did not reach out to find it.

Three years later, Joshua was born. Yes, he was another beautiful, easygoing baby and yes, he was a mommy's boy. He wanted me. And for the first time, I was scared to be alone. I asked my mom to stay longer. This time I knew something significant was wrong with me.

A mom from the boys' school called me one evening about a project we were working on. I was sprawled out on the floor in our master bedroom as I chatted with her. Josh was just a few weeks old, lying with Sanj on the bed, both sound asleep. She must have heard something in my voice, or maybe just felt God nudging her. She asked how I was doing. She understood something that I couldn't voice. As she listened

I poured out my fear that something was very wrong with me and I was afraid that I was going crazy.

She, herself a mom of five children who was studying to be a nurse, realized I was struggling. Postpartum "blues" seemed to be turning into clinical depression. I was in a deep dark place and did not know how to crawl out. Crying was a big part of my world. I finally went to my doctor and asked for the help I needed. I had a village of friends who jumped in, once I accepted that I could not do it all and that it was OK to admit this.

CHAPTER THIRTY-SIX

"Sometimes when things are falling apart
they may actually be falling into place."
—Unknown

The third week of July 2008 was sunny and hot. My boys were at a church basketball camp for the morning. It was free and fun, with lots of running around, which depleted some of my boys' never-ending energy.

It was Friday, the last day of camp, and I was getting three-year-old Josh out of the van to celebrate the week with the traditional BBQ for the kids and their families. As I took Josh out of his car seat and put him down and locked the vehicle, my cell phone rang. It was an unfamiliar phone number, something I would normally have just ignored, but this time I answered.

"Are you Reema Dixit?" a woman's voice asked.

Nobody ever addressed me by my maiden name. Before I could respond, she went on, "Are you Peter Dixit's daughter?"

My dad and I had been estranged for about ten years at this point. I continued to keep the boundaries I had put into place between him and my family, and truth be told, I had not missed him. Life was simpler without the uncertainties that came with him.

"Yes, I am Peter's daughter," I confirmed.

"I found your contact information in your father's wallet," she went on. I found myself pondering this later. My mom and brothers were still in my dad's life, to various degrees, while I was not. That fact that he had my cell number left me with emotions that were hard to dissect.

But I had no time to process that right now; the lady on the phone informed me that my dad was on life support and they were looking for the next of kin to make the necessary decisions.

Now I had to share this upsetting news with my mom and brothers. I grabbed Josh, who was trying to make a getaway while I was distracted, and then called Sanj. I was surprised to find myself bursting into tears as I told him about the phone call. How could I go, leaving my husband who worked full time, to care for our boys, ages three to thirteen, in the middle of summer? How was I going to get to Tennessee, where my dad was? And the bigger issue was: what was I going to do about my dad?

I had made peace with him over this time—or so I thought. Truth be told, I was going to Tennessee to bury him. I knew from my mom that he had been sick. While my mom did not agree with my decision to remove myself from my dad's life, she honored it. My mom and dad talked daily, yet there would be periods when my dad would simply ignore her, without explanation. She knew he was ill, but likely assumed the silence was his obstinance. The nurse I spoke to on the phone made it clear that they were only keeping him alive until the next of kin arrived. We were all shocked by this news; none of us had realized the severity of his illness.

Kumar told my mom about my dad's condition and made the arrangements for them to fly down to Tennessee. My brother Rajiv was living in Oshawa, about an hour away from me at that time. He and I were in the midst of being annoyed with each other, but when push came to shove, I knew we were in this together.

Rajiv and I drove all night, covering the ten to twelve hours from Toronto to Nashville, and arrived at about the same time as Kumar and my mom did. As I stepped into my dad's hospital room, I saw a man in the bed who bore little resemblance to my dad. He was bloated and his face was swollen. He had aged significantly in the last ten years and now looked like a shell of my dad. There were many tubes and contraptions that were obviously keeping him alive.

Kumar, standing next to my dad, told him that I had arrived. I started crying and left the room. Some of my tears were from shock, but I also felt deep sadness for him. My dad had given up so much happiness that could have been his had he simply let go of his pride and chosen his family. He had six amazing grandsons that he did not know. He had never even met three of my sons. My dad had made a life for himself in Tennessee that revolved around his church and the community. He was loved and appreciated in his corner of the world, but he was living a façade, because he had made the choice to turn his back on his family. I am sure that many of my dad's actions and choices stemmed from his mental illnesses but, sadly, I also believe some of his actions were based on his character.

We went to the waiting room. The silence was deafening as we sat there, numb. The doctor came and talked to us. My mom, always the nurse, asked the questions and listened as the doctor told her that my dad was only alive because of the machines. As we sat there, the pastor from my dad's church came by to see him. He greeted us, no doubt wondering where we came from and where we had been. My mom asked if he could anoint my dad.

Kumar and I were there only to bury our dad, clear his things out of his apartment, and be back by the end of the weekend to lives that did not stop for us. Rajiv had a closer relationship with my dad, though it was best described as a love-hate relationship. He stayed with my mom as Kumar and I went to find a funeral home and make arrangements.

Our plan was simple:

- Make arrangements
- Clean out his apartment
- Finalize things
- Go home

There was no emotion on that list. It was simply a series of things that needed to be done. A thousand and one feelings and thoughts flowed through me, but I pushed aside my nauseous stomach, pounding head, and skipping heartbeat. I had to deal with the tasks at hand.

We were in a waiting room back at the hospital when my dad's younger sister from Orlando walked in. She was his only sibling here in North America; the rest were in India. Lots of tears and hugs were exchanged; more tears flowed as my cousin, who was like a brother to me, came in with his partner. They had both flown in from Texas to support us, knowing this would be a highly emotional time.

My mom stayed at the hospital with my dad. The pastor came and did the anointing. My aunt and uncle stayed to keep my mom company.

We went to my dad's place the next day and began getting rid of his belongings. He lived like a squatter and his apartment was highly disturbing. His sofas were ratty, like something you would find on a curb waiting to be dumped in a garbage truck. Every part of his apartment was filled with mismatched, useless stuff—he was not quite a hoarder, but perhaps close to becoming one.

My dad still had the habit of making videotapes, then making numerous copies and passing them along to virtually anyone. He made numerous copies of my wedding video; sometimes I still find copies here and there. He would copy a preacher's sermons and give the videos to whoever would accept them. He had hundreds of poster pictures of Jesus's second coming or children sitting on Jesus's lap, and piles upon piles of religious magazines and pamphlets.

He had many new, unopened packs of undershirts and underwear. There were many, many packages of toilet paper. There were packs of the index cards he loved to use and always carried in his shirt pocket along with his four-colored pen. There was an excess of everything.

My dad had always cried poor, but this was not really true. He certainly used food stamps for some of his groceries, but his pantry was also full of expensive canned vegetarian food that he bought from the church's health food store. Sometimes he would mail a box of these canned goods to Kumar in Maryland. The shipping cost must have been astronomical.

Some of the things we uncovered in his apartment made us laugh.

We had a lot of fun going through his unique wardrobe, which included a bright, almost fluorescent blue suit, along with a bubble-gum pink suit! We wondered where in the world he found these things.

Mostly, though, it was shocking to see into my dad's life. When we were younger, he definitely displayed severe characteristics of OCD and had a place for everything. He kept his own pair of scissors in a very specific place and always seemed to know if we kids used them. He hated books not being perfectly aligned. Remembering how orderly he had once been made seeing his current living conditions all the more frightening, overwhelming, and heartbreaking.

Perhaps saddest of all were the pictures of my mom that were everywhere, with flowers added to the bottom and the caption "My Beautiful Wife." His obsession with my mom was frightening. A huge framed picture of her hung over his bed. I cannot imagine how much money he spent enlarging and framing it.

As we came and went from my dad's apartment, I realized he was somewhat of a celebrity in his building. He was a sort of unofficial "banker" for his apartment. If people were short on cash, he would lend it to them, until their welfare checks came in—and he would charge them interest. If they needed a ride to the doctor or the grocery store, he would give them one in his junker and charge his fee. Everyone seemed to know and love him, and everyone we met asked about him.

That evening we all left the hospital and headed to our hotel to try to get some sleep. We were all physically exhausted, not to mention emotionally drained, and in that state we didn't trust ourselves to make any big decisions.

As we got out of the car, my mom walked over to me—there in the hotel's parking lot—and wrapped her arms around me and sobbed. That moment was awkwardness defined. I did not want to be a support system to anyone. No one. The only person I wanted in that moment was my husband, and he was hundreds of miles away.

My feelings about her were complicated enough as it was. Now this! I was not sure I could do this. I knew I didn't want to do this. Where were my brothers? Why were they not doing something?

My mom's grief upset me. Why was she reacting this way? This man beat her senseless, abused her in every way a person could be abused—yet she still felt something for him, apart from anger? It seemed to me that she felt empathy, sadness, fear of losing this man, denial, grief, and the desire for a miracle. Where was that one emotion that was missing? Where was her anger? This man had hurt her children!

As my mom held onto me, sobbing, all I felt was frustration that she was turning to me, once again, to be her support. I was so angry that my mom could not just be furious with this evil human being. She was fighting for him!

I will never forget that moment as my mom clung to me, weeping. I looked at Kumar, my eyes saying a million things. His only response was a shrug. No matter how old you are, when in your parents' company it is easy to revert to your childhood roles. I never had the opportunity to truly be a child and I resented it.

My brothers never had issues with my mom. She showered affection and comfort on them and they reciprocated it. But for me, her touch was upsetting. What I craved was my dad's touch—the feeling of my hand in his hand, crossing the street or sitting next to him, finding comfort in his closeness. Long ago, on the weekends or whenever we were allowed, my brothers and I loved making our beds on my parents' floor. In the morning we would all find our place on their bed, and my favorite spot was lying next to my dad, embraced in his arms. I felt cherished in those moments.

We made arrangements for our dad's funeral. He was to be cremated and his church would host a memorial service. I had no intention of staying for the service. I hated being there; I missed my family, my home, my life, and I couldn't imagine attending a service that celebrated my dad's life. How could I attend a service where others showered praise and love on my dad?

My dad's doctor had suggested taking him off life support, telling us that if he lived he would likely be in a nursing home with no quality of life. My mom struggled with the decision to pull the plug, but I didn't understand why she found it so difficult to make the obvious decision. Kumar got a second opinion from a friend who was a doctor and based on her advice and the pressure she felt from us, her children, my mom finally agreed with the decision to have my dad taken off the drugs and the life support.

As we sat in the waiting room, after the doctor had left us, I was surprised that my tears did not come. My mom and both my brothers had tears rolling down their cheeks, but I felt emotionally constipated. I just wanted this to end and the plug to be pulled. We expected that once this was done, he would soon pass away. This allowed my mom and brothers time to say their goodbyes. I had no intention of going into that room again. I had said goodbye to my dad a long time ago.

We left my mom at the hospital, by my dad's side, where she wanted to be, while we went to finish working on our dad's place. After a few hours, Kumar returned to the hospital to encourage my mom to leave for a bit, to rest and eat. Shortly after arriving at the hospital, Kumar called me and said, "You better sit down."

He said, "Dad is awake, sitting up, and cognizant. You better come now." My brother loves being a prankster, and I rolled my eyes, annoyed that he thought this was a great time to be funny. But he assured me he was not joking.

Other than anxiety, I don't recall my emotions on the ride over. I had not come to see my dad alive. I lacked the emotional energy to do this. What in the world had happened?

I walked into his room. My dad was sitting up, looking normal (whatever "normal" was), and smiling. He had tears in his eyes and he looked so surprised and happy to see me. None of that felt good. It had been ten years. It was not the happy reunion that the visual might have suggested. I felt tricked. This whole thing was not what I had come for. I had left my family, left Sanj dealing with the chaos created by my abrupt departure in the middle of summer. I had my "Daddy" package all wrapped up, with a bow, tucked away in a place that did not affect my emotions. Now that neat bow was unraveling.

My mother was so happy. She believed that the anointing had saved my dad, and God was giving him another chance to fix things.

My mom chose to stay in Tennessee to help my dad get settled after his near-death experience. Again, I felt frustrated and angry at my mom for the choice she was making. My dad had so much control over her. She always said, "If I don't help him, who will? I can't just leave him like this." My mom was easily manipulated by him, or maybe had a connection with him that I would never understand. When she called me later, complaining about my dad, I told her it was her decision to stay.

While I didn't expect much, I decided to be receptive to any effort my dad made. Perhaps being at death's door had caused some sort of change.

My dad wrote me various letters over this period of time. In one he explained that he had made a deal with God. He loved his wife so much that if she was not in heaven, then he did not want to go either. He explained in another letter that my mom had told him to stay away from her. He loved her so much that he gave up his relationship with his children and grandchildren for her. This was the sacrifice he made for her because of his undying love. My dad lived in a different world, one that suited him. He blocked out any recollection of the abuse he inflicted on us, vehemently denying that he ever hurt us.

CHAPTER THIRTY-SEVEN

"Loving ourselves through the process of owning our story is the bravest thing we'll ever do."
—Brené Brown

Life went on for each of us after we watched my dad cheat death, but my life never went back to what had been normal. I started suffering from strange episodes that scared me, especially since I did not know how to explain them. A dream or scenario would play out in my mind, and when I was "in it," it made sense. Trying to remember it, after "coming out of it" found me unable to make sense of it. It recurred, with the same scenario playing out over and over.

What was happening to me? I was so frightened that I was losing my grasp on reality. Desperation gave me courage to seek medical advice, hoping I would not be admitted to a mental hospital for losing my grasp on reality. I prayed fervently to God for help and courage. As soon I mentioned what was happening to me, my doctor immediately said, "Oh, you are experiencing depersonalization." He made it sound normal, as if I had strep throat.

The Mayo Clinic describes depersonalization this way:

"Depersonalization-derealization disorder occurs when you persistently or repeatedly have the feeling that you're observing yourself from outside your body or you have a sense that things around you aren't real, or both. Feelings of depersonalization and derealization can be very disturbing and may feel like you're living in a dream."[2]

I sometimes had depersonalization episodes while driving, and while it didn't affect my driving, it was stressful. I usually pulled off to the shoulder and waited for it to pass. I hated explaining this to my children. As much as I tried to make light of it, I knew they were alarmed to watch their mom go through something that made no sense. The fear of the next attack seemed to usher in another delightful visitor—panic attacks.

These days, "panic attack" is a term used lightly in casual conversation, but those who have experienced true panic attacks never take them lightly. My heart raced, pure panic took over, and I felt like I was not going to survive.

My life seemed to be consumed by these ugly episodes and I felt helpless. My doctor became like family to me, as I was in his office far more often than ever before. I shed a lot of tears in his examination room, tears brought on by hopelessness and fear. I began the elusive game of trying to find the right combination of medicines that would help me. I was grateful to eventually find a pill that worked, though I learned that with time the dosage might need adjusting.

I am not a creature of habit—I have a hard time sticking to things that are regularly scheduled each day. I would often go to bed and forget to take my pill, or I would convince myself that skipping one day would not matter. I would still feel fine if I missed one or two days,

2   (https://www.mayoclinic.org/diseases-conditions/depersonalization-derealization-disorder/symptoms-causes/syc-20352911)

but I learned the hard way that after three days I was in trouble. On the third day without my medication I would just drop! I would fall so low and find myself spiraling downward quickly.

I did this one weekend and sat in the parking lot of the pharmacy without enough physical or mental energy to open my car door. I did not want to live like this. I simply wanted to die. Death. It seemed to be my only answer. What life was I giving my family while they watched me struggling with panic attacks that seemed to overtake my world? I sat in my car crying my eyes out. I begged God to help me. I felt so alone.

I wish I could say that something awesome happened, but it did not. I was frustrated with myself, knowing that my biggest struggle was the reality that I *needed* these meds to live the life I wanted. I hated that! This was and continues to be a struggle for me. I went into the pharmacy, crying as I told the young man behind the counter that I needed my meds. I verbally vomited all over him as he worked on my order. Ours was a small town, and the young man was a graduate from my boys' school. He saw the frenzied, tearstained woman before him, overwhelmed by emotions, and he simply talked to me calmly and with kindness, as if I were a sane, put-together lady asking for an aspirin.

I learned a hard lesson that day. I had recently been diagnosed with type 2 diabetes and I needed insulin to live. In the same way, I now understood that I suffered from a mental illness and I needed my meds to function. It was literally and figuratively a hard pill to swallow. I felt like this thing that was wrong with me was getting in the way of being the wife I wanted to be to Sanj and the mother I wanted to be to my six boys. I needed to find a way to accept my reality.

After returning from Tennessee, my "daddy issues" seemed to surface more than ever. I continued to yearn desperately for my dad's love. I wanted him to want me to be his little girl. I had been pretending for the last twenty years that I didn't care, but I wasn't a good liar. I missed having my dad in my life, but I knew I could not allow it as I had to protect my children.

One of my medical doctors was in the process of becoming a life coach, and she asked if I was willing to try something new. I agreed; I was desperate. She called it "Three Chairs."

My doctor/therapist placed three chairs in a triangle. One chair represented me, one represented my dad, and the other was representative of our relationship. Ugh! I sat in my chair and with my heart pounding, I told my dad that I loved him. Then I moved into the chair that represented our relationship and, squirming, I told him I wanted us to have a relationship, and I wanted him to love me like I needed him to.

Finally, I sat in the chair that represented my dad. Now I must make this disclaimer: I did not hear his voice or any audible voice. But as I sat in his chair, an indescribable feeling or sense washed over me. It was as if I felt him say, "I can't!"

It took some time for me to contemplate and process things, but I felt God opening my eyes to my dad's very specific, narrow love language. My dad did love me. He cut mangoes for us to enjoy rather than dealing with the peels. He bought little things he knew we liked, like cookies, and bigger things like that car I had in university. It was the best he could do and looking back it might as well have been a Mercedes. His love language was his way of loving me, and yet it was hard to see or appreciate because it was not normal.

With eyes that really sought the truth, I saw that my dad was broken. He had always been a duck out of water. When he went to India to visit his family, they had no idea how to cope with him. They wanted his trip to be kept short. My heart hurt for him. He had created a world for himself in Tennessee where everyone who knew him loved and respected him. Outside of that small circle, he was a misfit. He was weird. He was lost. My dad had social skills that only rose to a certain level, leaving him ill-equipped for normal, long-term interactions.

CHAPTER THIRTY-EIGHT

*"Forgiveness is not something we do for other people.
It is something we do for ourselves to move on."*
—Unknown

My brother Rajiv had moved to the Toronto area with his family. My brothers and I had each found unique ways of dealing with our dad. Rajiv wanted my dad to have a better life than the one we had seen in Tennessee, so he offered to bring my dad into his home, to be part of his family. It took convincing, but my dad accepted the offer.

Now my dad was living half an hour away from me. I felt such conflict. I knew that having him so close was just asking for trouble, but not wanting him to be near us felt wrong and selfish.

By this time, I had learned to use some tools to protect myself emotionally, and I knew my Sanj would never let anything happen to me. My dad was well aware of Sanj's strong dislike for him (to put it mildly). During this period of time, my dad and I had short interactions that were pleasant and easy. I had no expectations. I had a glimpse of what my life might have been like if this dad that I thought I saw now had been present for the younger me. But those wants and needs had long been buried. It was impossible to go back.

It struck me as absurd that at this point in his life, my dad would express horror at the abuse that took place in other people's homes. He would complain to me about a family member who was being violently abused by her spouse—as if he could not believe this could happen. He would ask me, "Can you believe how much he beat her?" or "You won't believe how he talked to her!" This baffled me. Did he really not remember?

Other times, he would comment on disciplining children, or how a parent talked to their child. He thought—now—that parents needed to lower their voices and acknowledge that the child made a mistake or did not know better. As I listened to him I was intrigued and baffled. I had read about selective memory and knew it was a real thing: one can train the mind to forget moments. When asked about a specific incident, my dad would actually seem to have no recollection and argue to the point of anger that it had not happened. Whether this was pretense or real, I couldn't tell.

Occasionally I would take my dad to run his errands. On one occasion I took him to the bank, and I was taken back by the affection and delight with which the teller greeted him. She remarked on what a lovely man he was and how lucky I was to have him for a father. Wow.

The encounter with the bank teller reminded me of an incident years ago that I had never forgotten. I was home for a weekend and we were leaving church when I noticed a little boy crying. He seemed to be all alone, so I started toward him. But before I could get there, my dad came out of the shadows, bent down, and picked up the little boy, murmuring words of comfort as the child settled in his arms. Soon he was reunited with his parents and my dad continued on.

How could my dad be so sweet, loving, and comforting to a stranger? How could he be so gregarious with the bank teller? How could this be true while with those who shared his blood, there was an impenetrable barrier of distance and violence?

I had long ago put my expectations away. I had learned to take what he offered, whether it was a bag of lychees or just a smile of appreciation. I tried to learn as much as I could about his younger days in India as well as about his family. I was learning that I could love my dad if I could accept his brokenness and know his love had been there, just not in a language I understood. He never did connect with our children, but that was partly my choice. By not having expectations of him, I never put him in a position where he could fail me again.

My dad eventually moved into a place of his own. He seemed happier that way. He was active in his church and well known by the church members. With his eclectic sense of style and penchant for vivid colors you could pick him out of the crowd sitting in church, no matter where he was. My dad had fallen into a rhythm in his life.

One afternoon I received a phone call. His landlord/roommate had found him facedown, dead on his bedroom floor. He must have had a heart attack and rolled off his twin bed and onto the ground. My dad was at rest and finally at peace. I was so grateful that God had finally taken him, and I was grateful for the hope that in heaven if we are reunited, my dad will be healthy and whole. He will be able to love me with all his heart. I will be able to feel his love. And he will finally be able to tell me, "I love you."

My dad was buried on my birthday weekend. I did not cry at his funeral. I didn't feel sad; I simply felt like I had been holding my breath and could finally exhale. He was at rest, and I could breathe. I did not harbor any ugliness or anger toward him. I was grateful to him for giving me life; I was grateful for the positive traits of his that I was blessed with. Finally, I had a peace that passed all understanding.

We chose to have the graveside ceremony (interment) with just family, but the memorial/funeral was for all those who wanted to pay their respects. My dad had worked with Rajiv to make all the funeral arrangements ahead of time, and we were grateful to Rajiv for doing that. True to form, my dad left detailed instructions as to what his eulogy would say and how to make the headstone just as he wished. It would be a closed-casket service.

Our three families gathered at the graveside, along with our mom. Kumar, his wife, and a couple of his children, along with me and some of my boys, were all at the site waiting for the rest of our families to make their way there. Without warning, Kumar walked over to the casket and lifted the lid! I screamed as I saw my dad lying there, wrapped like a mummy—his head so bloated and his face so white. Kumar's wife yelled at him, furious, as our kids were nearby. When asked why he did that, Kumar's reply was, "I wanted to make sure he was in there."

We were safe. We were all free, including my dad.

My dad had every opportunity to be loved, and yet he shrank from it. Love was a scary thing for him. To be loved, my dad had to make himself vulnerable. But as he lay in the casket, he was finally at peace.

CHAPTER THIRTY-NINE

"Crying is a way your eyes speak when your mouth can't explain how broken your heart is."
—Unknown

I realized later that the day my dad died my depersonalization episodes stopped completely. They had been a part of my reality for years, but I have not had one episode since that day. They were obviously connected to something that I associated with him.

There was still so much I didn't understand, and I often wondered if there was something about my dad that I was not remembering—something that my body would not let me remember. Perhaps it wasn't a memory, but some other powerful effect my dad had on me. Or maybe it was just the obvious reaction to years of emotional and physical abuse, and the stress that lingered into adulthood as my role in his life changed.

I assumed that with my dad's death, my body would find peace. I was wrong. Yes, the depersonalization ended, but there was more. Perhaps the tensions in my life, culminating in my dad's death, were like someone yanking on a chain. It is when the pressure is off and the force pulling on the chain suddenly disappears that the weak link finally breaks.

My dad died in September. My panic attacks began to increase in frequency just a few weeks later. The attacks affected my daily functioning and left me drained. This continued for several months.

In December, we took the boys to the Dominican Republic for Christmas. There would be no gifts this year; the trip together was their gift. What else did they really need? The boys were getting older, going off to school, finding jobs and girlfriends, all of which made a family vacation harder to coordinate. I was so happy and ready to simply relax. My panic attacks had been manageable for the last week or so, and I was looking forward to getting away from it all.

I was seated next to a young woman on the plane. I am a chatter, so unless my seatmate refuses to engage or acknowledge me, I will at least say hi and converse a little. She was delightful. During the flight, my panic attacks began to bombard me. I was panicking about my panic attacks. This sweet girl took my hand at one point and simply held it as we landed. No judgement. Simply kindness. She told me that she too suffered from panic attacks and could relate. I will never forget her act of kindness.

Sadly, the panic attacks were back in full force. The whole time we were on vacation, they didn't let up; they were a constant ugliness for me to reckon with. I tried so hard to simply breathe through them, to not let them control me, but when that feeling hit, it was hard to focus on anything else. I didn't understand it. This should have been a stress-free time.

The rest of the family had a great time. By day they played, ate, swam, snorkeled, and just enjoyed being together. The boys loved their time with each other, especially in the evenings and at night, probably doing things that I am sure Sanj and I would never want to know about. I love that they live by the motto "Brothers Stick Together," and I know they have stories they will share for a lifetime.

Still on vacation, I welcomed the new year with a continuation of the attacks. When we returned home, fatigue overtook me and living seemed almost too hard. Everything was hard. I couldn't stay alone. Fear consumed my life. Darkness was beyond frightening. I didn't even dangle my feet off the bed, as I couldn't be sure if someone was lurking under the bed, waiting to grab them.

Whenever I was alone I was petrified of a "boogie man" that I rationally knew didn't exist. I found that I couldn't be alone in the house when Sanj was at work and the boys were out. In the morning, I would go into the clinic with Sanj. If I was able to, I would work one of the front desks for a couple of hours, then crash on the floor in Sanj's office until he was done.

My girlfriends would pick me up, take me to one of their homes, and "babysit" me as I lay on their sofa and slept. They told me I would wake up and cry until I realized they were right there. Then I could go back to sleep.

My boys would finish school and pick me up from whatever form of "day care" I was in that day. Then Sanj would come home after work and take over.

All of this happened within the span of a few weeks, and it led my doctor to take significant action. I could not live like this, dependent on friends and family for the simplest things. My family had never known me as someone who was weak or incapable, and they were obviously very concerned. Whatever challenges life had thrown my way, I had always been determined not to let them affect my role as a mother, wife, or friend. I was the one who took care of others. Now I was reduced to this.

My doctor prescribed a strong sedative for me and suggested that I take this medication while under supervision, to allow my brain to reset and stop the frenetic craziness. It was like resetting a computer. Two of my dearest friends are a doctor and a nurse, and they took it upon themselves to help Sanj do this with me during the course of one weekend.

It still bothers me to this day that I have no recollection of the next few days—literally none. It's a very disconcerting feeling. I am told that during this period I was "hilarious." My friends know me to be unfiltered in the best of times, and apparently this medication led to an even greater lack of filtration. The result was rather comical. I am so grateful to have people in my life who are there when I need them.

The reset seemed to work. This missing weekend drained me enough to give me a fresh start. I did feel better and felt like there was hope that my panic attacks would one day disappear.

CHAPTER FORTY

*"A friend is one who overlooks your broken fence
and admires the flowers in your garden."*
—Unknown

My "reset" occurred in the month of January. In mid-February my second son Tyler, his girlfriend Alexx, and Alexx's mom Penny, who was one of my closest friends, asked if I wanted to go shopping with them for a prom dress for Alexx. I wasn't feeling up to it, but not wanting to be home alone, I agreed. Sanj and Zach were gone for the weekend. They were three hours away, in Ottawa, at a hockey tournament.

We drove about an hour into the city, stopped to eat, then headed to the stores. Alexx tried on a few dresses but didn't like any of them. We then went to the car, where, I am told, I started acting funny. Apparently, I began laughing to myself. They asked if I was OK and I responded that I was. I was in the backseat with Penny and Tyler was driving.

I am told that things quickly plummeted from there. My face went blank, as if no one was home. Penny, being a nurse, had a sense of what was to come. Soon after this I began seizing violently. She instructed Tyler to exit and pull into the gas station and call 911. I began flailing, punching, and fighting for my life. At one point I punched Penny in the nose and became very aggressive. Thankfully my seatbelt was on, which kept me in the vehicle as my feet were kicking out the window.

The ambulance arrived and the paramedics had to call for backup to assist. They initially assumed I was high on something and treated me roughly. At one point they literally had someone sitting on me while the others held me down. Tyler, who is everyone's protector in the family, can be very sensitive. Seeing his mother manhandled was too much for him; he marched up to the paramedics and informed them, "This is my mom. Could you be gentle with her? She's not normally like this."

Once the paramedics realized that I was not high and that this was a medical emergency, their approach toward me changed. I was very aggressive and impossible to control, so they shackled my hands and feet to the stretcher to protect themselves as well as me. They took me to the hospital nearby, where I was admitted into the emergency room and assessed. As all this was happening, I can only imagine what my poor Sanj must have been feeling as he made that three-hour drive to meet me.

Penny, Tyler, and Alexx later told me how I behaved while I was shackled. Apparently I begged the paramedics to release me so I could go to the bathroom. I had no interest in using the bed pan. It was painfully obvious that this version of me was not me at all.

It was a very long day and night for everyone. The doctors ran tests to try figure out what was going on. The CAT scan was inconclusive because they couldn't keep me still. I had to be heavily sedated just so they could manage me. For some reason the doctors assumed that I was epileptic, and no matter what Penny told them, they kept pursuing that path.

Partway through the night the emergency room was overtaken by someone in critical condition, so they moved me to a room where they kept those in police custody. This might have been disturbing to those with me, but I was completely unaware. When Sanj came, he found me with both hands and feet shackled to a gurney, with dishevelled hair, dressed in a hospital gown, and fitted with a diaper since the medical staff did not want to unshackle me to allow me to go to the bathroom on my own. However, my dignity was apparently still intact. I refused to use the diaper and kept pleading to use the bathroom. Eventually they did release me to use the bathroom.

When morning came a new doctor took over and asked Sanj how long I had been epileptic. Sanj reiterated that I was not epileptic. From that moment on, the doctors began investigating the seizure more specifically. I spent a few days in the hospital before they eventually released me. They still couldn't determine what had really happened. I have no memory of any of this; everything I know about those days I have garnered from friends and family.

In all of this, I see God's hand so vividly. Had I chosen not to go shopping with Tyler and my friends, I would have been alone with one of my younger children, who might not have been equipped to handle the emergency well. I wasn't driving because I was tired and had asked Tyler to drive instead. And I was with my dear Penny, who stayed calm and knew what to do.

Despite many tests and retests, nothing was found that could explain the seizure. My doctors and I believe that subconsciously, my body had just reached a breaking point. I had experienced multiple traumas in my life without ever pausing to address the pain. And now it seems my body had forced me to pause on its own accord.

I struggled even more after my seizure. Everything was so hard. I could not drive for six months because of the seizure. In addition to my irrational fear of the boogie man, I now had to manage the very real fear of another seizure! I was not me. I was not sure where I had gone, but this shell of a woman was not me. I cried a lot of tears. I slept for many hours. I found myself begging God to heal me. I could not live like this.

I was at church one day, partly because Sanj's team was singing but also because I still could not be left alone. I was scared. I was at my lowest ever. I had been robbed of my childhood. I had been abused instead of loved by my dad. I had been raped by someone I trusted. I had been beaten down so many times. I had refused to let those circumstances define me and had always found some way to get up, but now here I was, drowning. I felt like my life was just a mess, like I was wallowing in a cesspool. I was at rock bottom.

The last song was being sung. I could not find it in me to stand with the rest of the congregation. I didn't have an ounce of strength left to hold back my tears. In my head I shouted out to God, begging Him with all I was to please, please, please, heal my brokenness, as I could not live this way anymore, or ... for Him to just take me. He could do that. He could end it for me. If I was not to be whole and able to be there for my family, I asked God to simply take me. What I was doing now was not living.

I sat there, my shoulders shaking with grief and my tears cascading down my cheeks. I wept. I had nothing left. It was then that I felt an arm around me. I felt myself being held. Sally. This beautiful lady, whom I had known as an acquaintance all these years, had recently reached out to me. We were getting closer. I had shared some of my pain. She was an ER nurse. She was also, to me in that moment, an angel.

Sally let me weep. She prayed for me. She held me. The last song was sung. Penny and two others formed a circle around me. These ladies held me. They loved me. They prayed for me. I was not alone. I had an army of amazing people standing alongside me. They were not giving up on me, and God was not giving up on me. So I had to draw strength from these beautiful people and fight back. I had to find healing. I had to acknowledge the many wounds that were within me and find ways resolve my pain.

In that moment I saw something very beautiful. I had been hurt so hugely by my church but when I needed help the most, God used the women of my church to carry my pain.

It was a slow process. The panic attacks were still there. Every day was still really hard. But I was not alone. I had to accept that I needed more meds, one for anxiety and one for depression. I had to accept that I was broken, but I was fixable. I had not broken overnight, and I would not heal overnight. I had to be patient with myself. I had to have faith and trust that the God who had seen me through so much was not going to forsake me now. I had just discovered the true meaning of faith.

On the one-year anniversary of my seizure, I realized that my panic attacks had stopped. I was no longer scared of the "boogie man," and I was OK to be by myself! Sure, I locked all the doors, but that was OK. I found that one year later, I was stronger. I had been through a battle and lived to tell my story. I still had to take my meds to function, but I had accepted this as my reality. I had a good life, so if meds let me function as I wanted to, then I was OK with that. Mine was not a miracle in a moment, but God was still working miraculously in my life to bring peace and healing.

This period in my life was hard on our family. Up until that point, I had been the one who organized everyone's lives. My career was being a mom and I loved it. I loved my boys with all I had. The boys were active and every night seemed to find one of us chauffeuring them to various events.

When I got sick, life continued, but it took a turn. Now I was the one being taken care of. I was the one who my boys lay with until Sanj came home. It was my precious sons who would hold my hand when a paralyzing, irrational fear gripped me. God knew what my heart needed. He blessed me with my Sammy, Tyler, Jordan, Max, Zach, and Josh. I knew that I had to fight hard, even when it seemed impossible. I had to find my way back to these six beautiful creatures.

CHAPTER FORTY-ONE

"The pain you feel today will be the strength you feel tomorrow."
—Stephen Richards

During this year in which I was slowly getting better, other things happened that I now recognize as part of God's process of healing me.

Kumar and his family had moved to British Columbia, where he served as the ministerial director for the conference (a division of the Seventh-day Adventist Church). This meant he oversaw the pastors and leaders in that conference. He called me one night and asked if I would be willing to share my story of pastoral abuse at the ministerial meeting that he was organizing for ministers and church workers. I replied that I would be happy to.

I had always asked God to use this pain in some way, but after more than twenty years, nothing had yet happened. Now I felt a huge calling and excitement to share. Of course I also felt fear! I was not a public speaker. I would be speaking to a room full of pastors and church workers. I was to share my story and lead a workshop on this topic. How would I be received? Could I even do this?

I arrived at the church camp in Hope, British Columbia, which was surrounded by natural beauty that allowed me to momentarily forget my fear. Breathtaking! The first night I had no obligations and was able to simply take it all in. Most of the attendees seemed nice and greeted me warmly. Was this a BC thing, or was it because they realized I was Kumar's sister?

I slept well that night. The next morning, I led a workshop on "The Ten Steps a Perpetrator Takes, Steps to Protect Yourself as a Leader, and How to Minister to Someone Who Has Been a Victim."

I was nervous, but I had learned time and again that when God calls you, He will empower you. My workshop was held in a small boardroom that comfortably seated a dozen people, but that day people were crowded into the room and even in the doorway. My brother whispered to me that the keynote speaker had only three or four people in his group. This was not an arrogant observation, but rather a realization that this topic was one that was timely and relevant and so it was being embraced. Maybe, just maybe times were changing.

That afternoon I slept for two hours, with a peace that I had not felt in a long time. I was to speak to the group that night for worship and while I was, again, still petrified, I knew that God was holding me.

This was the first time I had ever shared my story in public. Anyone who looked at me could see that I was trembling. I am confident that God held me up physically and gave me the words to say. I found myself overwhelmed with emotion. I shared that in the last twenty-five years, I had just wanted someone from my church to care and say they were sorry. I wrapped things up by recognizing God's faithfulness in answering a little girl's prayer for a happy family. I ended with our family picture and then I sat down.

One of the awesome things God does is to place the right person with you even before you know you need them. My friend Sharon—the nurse who had come into the labor room and shooed everyone out for my privacy when I was having Sammy—was there. She was also a presenter at this conference, and she was the support I didn't realize I needed until that moment.

The conference president rose from his seat and took the microphone. He looked at me and said, "You want an apology from your church? I, as a minister of the gospel of the church, am sorry."

My friend Sharon held me as the tears flowed. Twenty-five years of heartbreaking pain was unleashed down my cheeks. I did not even realize how much I needed that. In that very moment, I knew that healing was taking place.

The incredible thing was that probably 95 percent of the pastors present came to me at some point and apologized to me too. What an example this leader was. He exemplified Christ. He may not have even realized the profound effect of his actions. I was approached by some who whispered that they shared my experience of sexual assault and abuse and that my story was their story. Some of them had never shared their story with anyone.

When God intervenes so powerfully, the devil often tries to get in the way. There was indeed foolishness that followed, but I only care to waste a few sentences on it. In a crazy small-world scenario, the keynote speaker for that weekend, whom I'll call Eddy, was someone who had been in the principal's office when BR was confronted by the principal all those years ago.

Initially, I thought it was awesome that Eddy was the keynote speaker and connected to my story. He had reached out to me with what appeared to be genuine support. But as I learned over the years, there are often two sides to a face.

Months later, while I was writing, I was researching my rapist for my story. I knew that he was often a guest speaker at churches in the area where he lived and he seemed to be as loved and cherished as he had always been. His secret was still unknown, obviously. He was still in ministry, now working as a chaplain for a group of hospitals, one of which was a children's hospital. Frustration had eaten at me over the years, but I had learned that there was not much I could do.

As I continued to search, I noticed that BR was preaching at a church that seemed familiar to me. I realized that Eddy, who had heard my story and reached out to me just three months earlier, was the pastor of the church where BR was invited to speak.

I felt immense betrayal and pain, as if I was being raped all over again. Here again, I was betrayed by a pastor.

Beyond upset, I called Sanj. Tears and heartache, emotions far too familiar, filled me. I shared my discovery with Kumar, too, who helped me pen this email:

> Hi Eddy,
>
> This is Reema (Dixit) Sukumaran, Kumar's sister—I spoke at the ministerial conference in BC—where you were presenting too earlier this year.
>
> I stumbled upon this video of BR speaking at your church—April 2—just last month.
>
> I was surprised (and hurt) to see he would be invited after everything I told you. He has never asked for forgiveness or accepted responsibility. Can you help me understand why he was invited to speak at your church?
>
> Thank you for your time,
>
> Reema Sukumaran

His reply:

> Hi Reema: First of all, I sincerely pray life is going well for you and your incredible family!
>
> Whereas I now count you as a friend, BR is still a friend as well, even as my two friends had a major, terribly painful situation that happened between them, where one wrongfully and deeply wounded the other.
>
> BR, as my friend, understands presently and historically my strong views on his bad choices he made some years ago and the pain he caused. But my friendship and care never change toward ANY of my friends whatever their failures in life. I choose to be loyal in that way. And yes, that failure and wrong is something he has to live with in his heart—the rest of his life.
>
> My care for you, Reema, is strong as well. But with all those I call friends, none will ever presume to determine what happens in my professional context. And with that said, BR was speaking for a conference-sponsored event which happen to be at my church. I wasn't even there. He was selected to speak by another group outside my congregation. Our church was just the host venue. He was not invited

by us. But if my church had invited him to speak, which we didn't, that is the prerogative of our congregation. I hope you hear both my heart and my mind.

I love you my friend and sister. And I care!

Eddy

I hate wasting words in my book about Eddy, as he was another pastor who was old-school and clearly part of that Boys' Club. But God used that experience to further my healing, though I wasn't able to see it at the time.

CHAPTER FORTY-TWO

"Pain is real, but so is hope."
—Jimmy Dooley

The arrogance of Eddy's email infuriated me. I shared my frustration with my friend Sharon, asking her what the point was of being faithful to the church when nothing seemed to change? Money talked. Was God directing me to sue the church? This was something I had thought of over the years. During these moments, I felt like I was expending emotional energy that I did not have to spare.

Sharon asked me to talk to a friend of hers. This friend, Grace, called me immediately, dropping what she was in the midst of and listening to me for more than an hour as I shared my story and my pain. I learned that she was the lawyer for the church in Canada. First and foremost, though, she was a person of integrity, and saw right and wrong even if it was the church that was in the wrong.

As I said, God works in mysterious ways. The leadership of the Canadian Union took it upon themselves, despite the fact that my rape did not happen in their country, to provide me with counseling. The counselor that I began working with was a gift to me. Over the three years we have worked together, the church never once questioned the time I have needed. I learned to approach issues that I had buried because they were too overwhelming for me and I did not know how to tackle them. I was taught skills to deal with things that continued to affect my daily life, things that the younger me would have run from. I learned to have empathy for the younger me, that girl for whom I had so much disdain. I learned to forgive her for things I saw as weakness, realizing that the younger me was stronger than I gave her credit for. She survived. I survived.

It's an exciting journey I've been on as I learned to see myself in a new light. I've finally learned to love the younger me, as well as the woman I am today.

I saw that while there is still a generation of pastors and leaders that treated the church as a Boys' Club, today's leaders and pastors are embracing and demanding change. The Seventh-day Adventist Church in Canada, later in conjunction with the North American Division, created a course educating others on "Sexual Abuse: Reclaiming Hope." I shared my story through a video that was used in the course. I was humbled as God continued to use my story.

The North American Division had joined and embraced the #MeToo movement in educating others as well as reaching out to victims. I was privileged to share my story at the 2018 #ENDITNOW conference that was facilitated by the North American Division of the church. More than ten thousand people heard my story and more importantly, were educated and challenged to be part of the change.

The president of the North American Division met with me and Sanj. He listened to me. I felt tears of anger leaking from my eyes as I shared my frustration. Annoyed, I told him, "These aren't sad tears; they're angry tears."

His response was simple: "They are still tears."

Sanj and I left his office with hope restored that this organization, which I have loved for so much of my life, is by my side. There are godly people within it who are willing to be led by Him. The Boys' Club is slowing dying, and God is showing me that He's got me, just as He always has.

Shortly after this, the Ford vs. Kavanaugh hearing came to public attention in the United States. As part of the questioning during the hearing, several people asked how Christine Blasey Ford could remember some details of her assault and not others. Part of her response was, "WE DON'T FORGET!"

This questioning infuriated me. I started to write BR a letter about how I had not forgotten. Sanj suggested that it would be more meaningful to post it on my blog, rather than sending it to BR.

WE DON'T FORGET

- *It has been 9,635 days since you raped me.*
- *It has been 9, 635 days since you violently took my virginity from me.*
- *It has been 9,635 of my dealing with the repercussions of your evil act.*
- *It has been 9,635 days of understanding how such a betrayal could occur.*
- *It has been 9,635 days of wondering how a "man," a father, a husband (at the time), a supposed "man of God" could violate another human in such a way.*
- *It has been 9,635 days of wondering how someone could profess to care about the pains and hurts of one and then use that information to his advantage.*
- *It has been 9, 635 days of my questioning what did I do? Was this my fault?*
- *It has been 9,635 days of trying to understand what kind of father would violently rape a young woman (period) and then do so with his child in the bathtub next door.*
- *It has been 9,635 days of wondering if you know you are a sick person.*
- *It has been 9,635 days of wondering if you realize you are a narcissist.*
- *It has been 9,635 days of wondering how the leadership of the church I belonged to and loved could turn its back on me.*
- *It has been 9,635 days of wondering if your wife knows the truth.*
- *It has been 9,635 days of wondering if your children have any idea of the vileness of their father.*
- *It has been 9,635 days of feeling sorry for the thousands of people you have reached, knowing you are betraying them too.*

- *It has been 9,635 days of feeling sorry for the leadership and friends who did not hold you accountable and yet knowing they will face God, at the ultimate judgment.*
- *It's been 9,635 days of me struggling, sometimes just surviving, as my body deals with the repercussions of someone physically pinning me down and forcing his being into my most sacred of places.*
- *It has been 9,635 days of constantly looking over my shoulder.*
- *It has been 9,635 days of fearing being anywhere alone with a male. Riding an elevator, going to my car in a garage, putting out the garbage in the dark are things that haunt me constantly.*
- *It has been 9,635 days of fighting PTSD, panic attacks that take over, or just uncurling from the safety of the fetal position, all exhausting.*
- *It has been 9,635 days of screaming out at the memory of ultimate betrayal. I trusted you. You made me trust you.*
- *It has been 9,635 days of wondering who else, how many others?*
- *It has been 9,635 days of waiting and hoping that time heals all wounds. Yet realizing some wounds leave a huge, ugly scar that will be felt every day.*
- *It has been 9,635 days since my view of this world changed forever. I believed that most people had good in them. And yet, you proved me wrong.*
- *It has been 9,635 since my colorful world became black and white.*
- *It has been 9,635 days.*
  Tomorrow it will be 9,636 days.

My rage and fury poured out. I have been reminded of this vile act every day of my life since I was raped. WE DON'T FORGET! I can tell you where the furniture in the room was, though it is blurred, but if you ask me about the details of the brutality of that horror, I can vomit moment by moment to you.

WE DON'T FORGET! Yet trust me, I have wished every day that I could.

An amazing thing happened. The post got traction. It was shared on Facebook. My brothers shared it. Students and people from that community reached out. They believed me. They remembered BR's gregarious, charming personality. They remembered his overly affectionate behavior. I was embraced in this incredible community of love. His lies were being revealed. This post was seen more than ten thousand times and reached others who had experienced ugliness too. Again, pieces of my brokenness were being healed.

CHAPTER FORTY-THREE

"Sometimes the most beautiful people
are beautifully broken."
—Robert M. Drake

My mom and the three of us, her children, were always close, maybe because we had experienced so much together. She had been struggling with her health for a while, and she was eventually diagnosed with idiopathic pulmonary fibrosis.

The Mayo Clinic defines pulmonary fibrosis as a lung disease that occurs when lung tissue becomes damaged and scarred. This thickened, stiff tissue makes it more difficult for the lungs to work properly. As pulmonary fibrosis worsens, it leads to progressive shortness of breath.[3] It is common in heavy smokers, but my mom never smoked a day in her life.

The long and short of this disease was that my mom was going to slowly suffocate to death. It was one of the ugliest ways to die. How did this happen? How could someone who had suffered so much her whole life have this as her ending? My mom was always a fighter. So much of life had been a struggle for her. How fair was it that the last bit of life would be a struggle too?

Not being in the medical field, my brothers and I were able to avoid the reality of her condition for a while. Sanj would often bring it up and ask if we really understood, but I think a part of us was in denial.

---

3 [https://www.mayoclinic.org/diseases-conditions/pulmonary-fibrosis/symptoms-causes/syc-20353690]

Kumar and Rajiv were living in British Columbia with their families. My mom had been on her own in Maryland for about three years and had a lot of support from her friends and family there. She had always been everyone's caretaker. She helped her friends and family learn how to access help from the government when they were eligible for it. She cooked and provided food for those who needed it. She was a doer. She didn't know how to sit still, and she didn't let her diagnosis stop her. Once she was on oxygen, she would take her tank with her and continue to do her thing.

Kumar and his family moved back to Maryland—a timely move, as by this time my mom needed more support in order to continue living on her own. God has His way of working for our good, and looking back, we were able to see His direction.

My mom did well for the first two years after her diagnosis. After that, her illness progressed rapidly. I began to fly down frequently to give her a hand and to give my brother a break for a few days. Kumar did so much for my mom, stopping by a few times a day to bring her things she needed or wanted. I will always be grateful to him and his family for all they did.

By February 2018 my mom's decline was significant. Sanj suggested that maybe I needed to move in with her, until the inevitable. After discussing this with my brother, we decided that this would be the best scenario, since my mom refused hospice and made us promise we would let her die at home.

I was clueless as to what I was jumping into, and I suppose that was a blessing. My mom was on full-time oxygen. Kumar had taken a job as a hospice chaplain. Again, funny how God works. This was not something my brother had ever thought of doing, and yet when the job came up, it seemed to have his name all over it. Working for hospice, Kumar learned all that hospice could offer my mom. She was able to receive care at home, and I did not have to step into a nursing role that I was not trained for.

When I first arrived, she was still in "mom mode." She would drag her oxygen tubing to the kitchen to make me something she knew I liked. But within a few days, this was no longer possible. She loved her court shows on TV, so we watched them together. I was shocked at how addictive these shows became. At 11:00 a.m. there was a show about paternity testing. We got annoyed when the hospice person came for her daily caretaking and interrupted the show! My mom also loved the Hallmark channel. She seemed to know all the movies and as we watched she would tell me the story.

At other times she would talk non-stop about her childhood, her dad, her mom. She would talk about my birth and how special it was. She told me how my dad was so excited when I was born that, without really thinking it through, he picked me up and started to walk home with me.

She would praise me, bragging to her friends that I was an amazing daughter who had left everything, my husband and boys, to be there for her. I felt like a fraud. I was not amazing. In my heart I resented having to do this. But my mom needed me—and more importantly, wanted me—by her side. Usually she would have said, "No, I'll be fine. The boys and Sanj need you." Not this time.

"Mom, I am going to stay," I told her.

"Thank you so much. But how long can you stay like this?"

"As long as I need to," I told her.

I set up a mattress in the little living room in my mom's apartment. From where I lay, I had a view of her on her hospital bed. My mom was very concerned that I would be there alone when she passed. I had never been around death and my mom was very aware of my squeamishness. I, too, was concerned about the possibility that my mom might die alone in the middle of the night. My brother lived twenty minutes away and I knew he would be there in a heartbeat if I needed him, but I was alone with my mom, who was very sick.

My first three nights there, I was petrified. I could not sleep and I found myself constantly listening for my mom's continued breathing. She moaned constantly, so when she was quiet, I would hold my breath and pray really hard. I would call Sanj if it wasn't too late in the night and I would go check on her while I kept him on the phone.

On one of my first mornings with her I did not hear her breathing, and I was scared. I stood in her doorway, straining to see if her chest was moving. I took a picture and sent it to Sanj, telling him I didn't know if she was dead. He texted me at the same moment that I noticed it too—her oxygen tube was up on her forehead!

I rushed to her side, with Sanj still on the phone. "Mom? MOM?!!"

She moved! She opened her eyes with her usual fearful look, then smiled at me. "Mom, your oxygen tube is on your forehead!!!" I put it down under her nose. She laughed. She told me that it must have just happened, or she would have begun to cough.

Like many nurses, my mom was a nightmare of a patient! She had her own ways of doing everything. Any major movement caused a coughing fit and she struggled to breathe. She would ask me to massage her throat in the neck area. She found comfort in Starburst candy; apparently the chewing and swallowing gave her comfort, as did her caffeine-free Diet Coke. While we had our misgivings about this irrational approach, it seemed to give her comfort. My mom had her pulse oximeter on her finger or right by her side constantly checking her blood oxygen levels. Being a diabetic, she would check her sugars endless times a day. She was in palliative care and did not really need to monitor her sugars or check her oxygen levels, but I realized this was her comfort. She must have found reassurance knowing that she could still regulate her sugar and take her meds. She was still fighting.

This disease had no timeline. She could live for months or die that night. I found myself panicking often, calling Sanj, crying my eyes out, telling him I could not do this! I did not understand why God was asking this of me. Why was this my mom's ending? Sanj was always there. Sometimes he would say the right things and other times he would just listen, knowing there was really nothing to say.

As the days passed, I found myself fearing that I was going to break again. I told Sanj I was worried my mental health would regress. I arrived at my mom's apartment during the week of my one-year anniversary of my seizure, a year when my whole world was lost to me and God offered healing. It had been a year of healing while my panic attacks were slowly abating. While I didn't realize it at the time, it was right around this time when my mom needed me that my last panic attack occurred and many of my fears subsided. But in the moment,

I just felt so fragile, like I was going to break! But again, what God asked of me, He prepared me for.

For many years, I had wondered why my mother's touch upset me. She loved hugs and snuggles from my boys and her other grand-children. I alone withheld this loving touch from her. Was I punishing her? That was not like me.

Looking back, I see that God was giving me time to mend this pain. I wanted my mom to protect me when I was a child. I wanted her to stand up for herself. I wanted her to fight for our happily ever after. I wanted my mom to use those hands to love me in the way I needed. I had huge hurts, and I blamed a lot of that on my mom.

Kumar would come and hug her or hang over her chair or just love her with his touch. But even when he was there, it was me she would ask to rub her neck when she was trying to get her breath back. I would sit there massaging her neck, shoulders, and back as I stared my brother down. Was this really necessary?

Sanj came to visit and watched with concern as I touched my mother. He was shocked and disturbed, because he was aware of my aversion to touching or being touched by her. He wondered out loud if I was OK. Was I OK? I had to really process that. For so many years, my mom's touch had been upsetting to me. I am not sure I really understood my aversion to it, aside from associating her touch with her stifling emotional dependence on me, which I resented. Yet now, as I sat with my mom day and night, I just knew that massaging her neck was beneficial because it calmed and relaxed her. I realized my touch seemed to comfort her like nothing else could. I am sure this was a change God worked on my heart. I was asking God to help my mom. And here He was showing me how to help her while allowing healing for me too.

The uncertainty of the situation overwhelmed me. We had no idea how long she would live. How was I going to commit to this without knowing how long I would be away from my family, my world? I had to find a way to function that wasn't powered by fear.

It is amazing how God gives you the strength to handle what is placed in front of you. I found myself crying all night long, begging

God for strength; I begged Him to not let me break down; I begged for my boys to be given what they needed through this time, as they adored their Amamma. I asked God to give Sanj what he needed as well and looking back, God answered all those prayers!!!

The song, "Do It Again" by Elevation Worship became my anthem. Sanj would play it for me, reminding me that God can and will "Do It Again." He will not fail us, even though we forget how many times He has rescued us. The song became a source of strength as it declared God's promises. Every time I hear that song, I'm softened by gratitude, knowing that God answered prayers and held us all up.

Nights were hell. Mom would fall asleep by 11:00 p.m., and I would start crying as soon as she did. My heart was breaking. I missed home so much. I needed Sanj right there with me. I did not know how I was going to watch her die.

I was texting Sanj one night, pouring my heart out. I knew he would not see it until morning, but just texting him made me feel close. My tears blinded me; I was gasping as I wallowed in my ugly cry, words of fear, grief, anger, and brokenness spitting out on my phone. Then I heard something. A ping! Sanj was replying!

I was shocked. "What made you wake up?" I texted. He never wakes up. He sleeps like a rock!

He replied, "I don't know. I just woke up."

I knew then that though we were going through an ugly time, I was being held in God's hands. Sanj slept with the phone beside him so that when I needed him at night, he could be there for me. God had me. God had us. All of us.

I still hated it. I still found myself screaming, "WHY, GOD?!!!" Why would my mom not die peacefully? How was it fair that my dad was allowed to keel over and die suddenly, while my mom had to suffocate to death?

As the weeks passed, a slow change began to take place in my life. I listened to my mom share her stories, her hurts, and her joys. I learned that in so many ways I was very much like her. I do not say this to take away from my brothers, as she adored them, but in my mom's life, it seemed that there was a need only I could fulfill. Maybe it was complete trust, maybe I was her best friend, but she had a special connection with me.

As we spent those long days together, as she talked about my children with pride and love from those years when she lived with us, my irritation slowly dissolved. I began to understand that this time with her was a gift, one that I did not even realize I was both giving and receiving.

We got into a routine of sorts. Looking back, I know that I was blessed with time to heal my own heart. Hour by hour, day by day, my anger and hurt began to melt. My heart started to bleed. As I watched her trying so hard to get oxygen into her body, I found myself unable to breathe. My hands reached out to grab her worn tired hands—the same hands that had worked so hard to do her best for us. When I reached for her hands, my heart started to feel lighter. My heart was beginning to let go of anger; I was slowly letting the walls fall down. I was holding her hands, willing my strength into her.

Acts of kindness are a big part of my mom's love language. Now, I was speaking that language to her. We looked at old pictures; she told stories of my boys. She loved them so much. I realized how much sharing my life and my children's lives allowed her to experience a piece of my Cinderella story, my happily ever after.

As the days passed, her condition deteriorated quickly. Her sister-in-law came once a week, despite her own health issues, and spent time with my mom. This gave me a break, often one I did not want or think I needed, but for which I am ever grateful. My mom's friends kept in touch too; one friend in particular called every day at 9:00 a.m.—every single day! She would grab something and bring it over if my mom needed or wanted anything. My mom was blessed with such beautiful support.

Kumar still stopped by daily, bringing me food and making me go out for a few minutes. Rajiv called my mom many times a day or FaceTimed her with his children from British Columbia.

As breathing became harder for her, I found my own breathing labored. I told Sanj and my brothers I was catching my mom's disease. Of course, I was kidding, but as she struggled to breathe, my heart was breaking. I pleaded with God to please take this cup away from her, to let her have a heart attack and die in peace. I begged Him! It was so horrifying when she begged me to turn her oxygen up from eight to ten, the maximum it could go, and I had to lie and tell her I did it. She didn't realize that she had already been at ten for some time.

Sanj flew up again after two weeks. I needed him. I was so broken. He spoke to my mom in private before he left, letting her know he loved her and that he was grateful for all she did for all of us. My mom was so touched. She told everyone!

As my mom and I talked about our lives, she expressed remorse for everything she knew I had been through. She told me we were alike. We both had strength that others did not. She had first told me this years ago, and at the time it made me so mad!!! I ranted to Sanj that I was *nothing* like my mom. I didn't see her as being strong; if she had been strong, she would have left my dad. That comment haunted me over the years.

Now, I listened as my mom shared her happiness, her hurts, her belief in God, her love for her children, and her pure unconditional love for her grandchildren. I realized that there is another definition of "strong" that I had not considered before.

My mom had strength like no one I knew. She had been dealt a rotten hand. She never saw her beauty; all she saw was her darkness and what she perceived as ugliness. She never fell in love. The best thing that came from her being with my dad was her children. She never had wealth or worldly treasures but the hugs, drawings, and time with her grandchildren were worth more than anything else she could have wanted. My mom had strength to get up after literally being beaten down. She had strength to work harder than most ever do. She had strength to always lend a hand to whoever needed it. I never heard my mom complain about her life. She never questioned God. She had a faith unlike any one I have seen.

The following week, Sanj brought our six boys. They were aware that this was the last time they would see their Amamma. My mom seemed to draw strength from deep within as the boys surrounded her. She loved them as she always had, listening to them, laughing with them, staring into each of their eyes, drinking in their beauty. She had loved my boys with such a passion from the time she first laid eyes on each of them. There was nothing she would not have done for them.

It was time. The last goodbye. Each of the boys kissed her; she hugged them and told each of them she loved them. They left. My mom sat in her chair with the look of being in a faraway place, somewhere reality was not allowed.

The door opened again. My youngest, Josh, came back, saying he had forgotten something. He stared at my mom before he left. He had just come back to look at her once more. As we walked toward to the vehicle with tears pouring, he said, "Amamma looks so sad."

I looked at each of my boys as the brokenness that was in each of their hearts poured out of their eyes. They were blessed with such a gift. I was so grateful that they saw that. They loved her so much and she loved them back. No one spoke, but the vehicle was filled with the overwhelming sound of heart-wrenching sobs as these boys-to-men already felt the emptiness that would never be filled.

They went home; I stayed, helping my mom more and more each day. As her breathing became frighteningly labored, I found myself reaching for her hand more often. She squeezed it tightly. My mom was begging for my strength once more. During this time God had blessed me and healed my hurts, bitterness, and anger. My hand squeezed my mom's worn, tired hands, offering her all my strength, love, and gratitude.

All my pain had disintegrated as I realized that my mom had loved me through her love language. She had cooked constantly, no matter how many hours she had worked. She had bought me jeans and shoes I had coveted. She had spent whatever she needed to so that I would feel cool moving into my dorm. She beamed with pride when I marched down to receive my diploma from university. She had tears in her eyes as she hugged me before letting me leave her home for my own, knowing I was marrying a good man. She could not have been prouder when she held each of her grandbabies in her arms.

My mom's body ached. She always said she was fine, but as the pain took over, she could no longer lie. I squeezed lotion into my hands and massaged her legs. These legs that had held her up through so much over the past eighty-three years, had atrophied. Skin hung from her bones, dehydrated from the failed feeble attempts at eating even small morsels of food. I rubbed her arms, which had so long ago held me with delight. I remembered the hugs at my graduation, at my wedding, after birthing her grandchildren. I rubbed my love into her arms and legs. Tears filled my eyes as my mom said, "Oh, this feels so good. I have never been touched like this."

I love you. Our family did not say those three words very often. For some reason my mom seemed unable to say them to me. As my mom's end was in sight, I had a strong need to hear her say, "I love you." Sanj told me to just tell her or ask her. But that wasn't what I needed.

I tried once as I got her settled in her chair. "Mom, you know I love you, right?"

She replied, "Of course I do. You would never do all you are doing otherwise."

Darn! That was a miss!

On her last day, while she was still cognizant, I videoed short messages for each of her grandchildren and my brothers. She told each of them she loved them. My brother, Rajiv, was unable to make it before she died. Kumar and I FaceTimed Rajiv and my mom told him that she loved him. Her last words to him were, "I'll see you in heaven."

There came a day when I knew a transformation had taken place in my life. I can vividly remember making a decision to simply love this woman without expectation. Just hours after this epiphany, she in essence gave up, and we knew it. Hospice nurses came and organized things for her comfort. She had refused morphine until she knew it was the end. Kumar and I took turns sitting by her side. At 4:37 a.m. my mom became very agitated. She was heavily medicated but seemed to be desperately reaching out for us. Kumar and I sat on either side of her bed.

"We are here, Mom," Kumar reassured her.

"Mom, we love you," I said.

My mom, in her weakened state, hanging on to the last piece of her life here on earth, slurred, "I love you, too!"

I stared at Kumar, "Did you hear that?!"

My mom found her forever peace at 8:30 a.m. on March 15, 2018.

Tears flowed. My heart was in pieces as I looked at my mom, able to see so much of myself in her. We were both *Beautifully Broken.*

Made in the USA
Middletown, DE
10 December 2020